Flags and Standards
of the Napoleonic Wars

Compiled and drawn by Keith Over

BIVOUAC BOOKS LTD.

INTRODUCTION

It has not been my intention in compiling this book to attempt to give a complete encyclopedia for flags and standards of the Napoleonic era. Such an undertaking would produce an immense work running into several volumes and requiring a lifetime's research. This book contains information on the flags and standards of the main combatants of the Napoleonic conflicts. It is designed to be of interest to model soldier makers and collectors, diorama makers, and wargamers who wish to have their armies led by the correct colours.

I have dealt with the countries in alphabetical order for easy reference. The size of the sections dealing with the different countries varies greatly and there are several reasons for this. The main reason is that whereas some countries had a standard pattern with no (or only minor) differences between the designs for different units, others had individual patterns for just about every formation, Britain being among the latter. For this reason it has been necessary to severely edit the number of illustrations for such countries as they would individually demand a complete book in themselves. I have however included as much information and as many drawings as possible so that the reader will be able to deduce those designs not illustrated.

I have stayed strictly with flags and standards and have not gone into the various fanions carried as these too demand a study in themselves. Wherever possible I have used as reference actual existing items. It is evident from these relics that quality and design varied greatly, and often the devices were poorly drawn and painted on the silk or cloth. Central devices were often far from central or even upright. It is a great temptation when drawing these to straighten up the lines, sweeten curves and make circles actually circular. I have resisted this temptation as much as possible and attempted to show them as they were.

Keith Over 1976

ACKNOWLEDGEMENTS

My thanks go to all those who helped with the compilation of this book. In particular to Harry Kinna for the loan of material used in the Prussian section and to Otto von Pivka for the supply of material included in the sections on Sweden, Portugal, Anhalt, Baden, Brunswick, Hanover, Hesse and other German states. Last but not least my thanks go to Jan for the initial typing of my notes and general creature comforts.

Keith Over 1976

First published in 1976   © 1976 BIVOUAC BOOKS LTD.   SBN 85680.012.0

Published in Great Britain by
Bivouac Books Ltd.
21/25 Earl Street,
London, EC2A 2AL.

Published in the USA by
SKY BOOKS PRESS LTD.
48 East 50th Street,
New York, NY 10022, USA.
ISBN 0-89402-033-1

Printed in England by James Cond Printers, Birmingham.

TABLE OF CONTENTS

FRONT COVER

Top row, left to right.
France, Infantry flag Vistula Legion
Warsaw, Standard 1st Chassuers
Italy, Royal Guard Grenadiers.
Bottom row, left to right.
France, Infantry flag, 1815.
Russia, Guard flag, 1813.

Austria

In the infantry the Leibfahne was carried either by the Grenadier company (which in the Austrian army was detached from the parent unit and grouped together with the grenadier companies from other regiments to form an elite), or the 1st (Leib) battalion. The other battalions carried an ordinary flag each. Up to 1806 it seems likely that the grenadiers carried two flags (Leibfahne and one ordinary) but after this date only one was carried. In all companies the flag was carried by a Fahnenfuhrer.

From existing items it seems that there was no hard and fast rule as to the size of the flag. The flag of 1792 to 1805 as illustrated was approximately 132cm. by 168cm. The border 'flames' always had a curved edge and never straight as often depicted. For 1792 to 1805 the yellow and white 'flames' point inwards and the red and black outwards. The field of the main part of the flag was yellow and the eagle black. The crown was red and gold and the ribbons issuing from the underside blue with a gold border. The two smaller crowns, halos, beaks, orb, sceptre, feet, chains and monogram were all in gold. The ribbon holding the orders below the escutcheon was red and white. The coats of arms were coloured as per the 1806 shield in the colour section. The sword had a silver blade with a gold hilt.

The 1805 ordinary flag was coloured similar to that above. Size was approximately 132cm. by 176cm. The centre escutcheon was yellow (a lighter shade than the ground colour) with a black 'Doppeladler' crowned gold with golden feet, orb and silver bladed sword. On the breast of this eagle in turn there was the red and white national shield. The imperial crown rested on top of the major breast shield, and a holy crown in gold was in its place above the heads of the eagle.

The 1806 flag was of similar size to that of 1805 and is illustrated in the colour section. This pattern was carried until 1816. It should be noted that on this flag only the yellow 'flames' of the border pointed inwards. The pike head for all flags was gilt and the pole itself was painted in diagonal bands. The colours varied but were always combinations of red, black, white and ochre. Late in the Napoleonic wars the practice of adding the regimental title to the upper corner of the yellow field near to the staff in an abbreviated form began to be used.

The 'ordinary' flags and standards were normally painted on to yellow silk. The degree of draughtmanship employed in individual flags varied and many were quite crude in application. The two heads of the eagles were often different and the halos far from circular. More noticeable was that the whole of the eagle and central devices were sometimes off centre on the sheet, being either nearer the fly or pole.

The Leibfahne were usually better made and embroidered rather than painted. The infantry Leibfahnen were the same size as the ordinaries and were of white cloth. The flame borders were similar to those on the ordinaries with white and yellow (gold) 'flames' pointing inwards. On the one side was the image of the

Virgin similar to that on the cavalry standard. The gold scrollwork border was of oval shape and a semicircle of stars surrounded the Virgin's head. The space within the scrollwork was light blue fading to white in the centre behind the figure. The Virgin is in natural colours with blue and white robes. At the Virgin's feet are a serpent and globe in natural colours. On the obverse of the Leibfahne there was the double-headed eagle as per the ordinaries but on a white field. Honours were awarded in the shape of ribbons attached to the staff head.

The cavalry standards were generally scaled-down versions of the infantry flags. They measured approximately 80cm. by 80cm. The 1806 standard illustrated is similar to the 1806 infantry flag but the semicircle of shields was omitted. It is also interesting to note that the border was of the earlier pattern with both white and yellow flames pointing inwards. The Leibstandard seems to have been a little larger than the ordinary standard and the pattern was similar to that of the infantry. The Leibstandard was carried by the 1st or Leib squadron of a regiment. The standards were attached to a staff which was either plain black, plain ochre, or ochre and black diagonal stripes.

The Ehrenfahne (Honour flag) illustrated was issued to the 4th Hussar regiment, Hessen-Homburg, for services to the Pope, and was dated 1814. The field was white with fringe and border decoration embroidered in yellow. The Doppeladler was in heavy silver embroidery with gold crowns, chains, feet, orb and sword hilt. Sword blade was white. The lining to the imperial crown was red and the ribbons blue. Coats of arms were in their proper colours. Staff was ochre and topped by a large gilt star-shaped emblem.

1   Infantry flag 1792 to 1805.

5 Ehrenfahne 4th Hussar regiment 1814.

4 Cavalry Leibstandard.

3 Cavalry standard 1806.

2 Infantry flag 1805.

Anhalt

Anhalt-Lippe and the smaller German states of the 4th, 5th, and 6th Rheinbund-Regiments.

The smaller German states were in 1807 persuaded to join the Confederation of the Rhine. The contingents were grouped together to form the 'Rheinbund' regiments. Thus the contingents of Weimar, Gotha-Altenburg, Coburg-Saalfield, Meiningen and Hildburghausen formed together the 4th Rheinbund-Regiment, those of Dessau, Bernburg, Kothen, Lippe-Detmold and Schaumburg-Lippe the 5th Rheinbund-Regiment and those of Rudolstadt, Sondershausen, Reuss and Waldeck the 6th. A Bataillon des Princes was formed in 1808 with further contingents from Rudolstadt, Sondershausen, Reuss, Detmold, Schaumburg and Waldeck (this unit had no flag). Flags carried at this time were two by Gotha-Altenburg, one by Coburg-Saalfield (probably not on campaign) and one by Anhalt-Dessau. After several years of depletion through hard campaigning the regiments were reconstituted in 1812 for the Russian campaign. Two flags were carried at this time, one of the Anhalt battalion (presented in 1811) and that of the Lippe Battalion (presented in 1812), both being carried by the 5th regiment. The first measured 80cm. by 70cm. and the staff was white. The flag itself was white and bore in the centre the arms of Anhalt. These were to the right the arms of Saxony, green diagonal over black and yellow (gold) bands, to the left a red eagle displayed on a white background. Surround to oval was gold, as was the crown which also had a red lining. On the reverse was the word ANHALT in the centre. In 1811 a new flag was issued which was similar to the above described 1807 edition with the following difference—a ribbon of white with black lettering, bearing the word ANHALT, was draped across the escutcheon. The flag was the same on both sides.

The flag for the Lippe battalion, known as the Danzig flag, was of a pale yellow material. This colour was as per a description made in the 1830s and was possibly white originally, having discoloured with age. It measured 105cm. by 100cm. and was attached to a white staff 265cm. long which was topped by a gilt spear point. The diamond outline and the lettering were in gold and the coats of arms in their proper colours. These were for the one side:—
Upper fly red field, gold eight point star with black bird above (Schwalenberg).
Upper staff white, three blue wavy lines based with red (Ameide).
Lower fly arms of Saxony.
Lower staff a blue field with gold displayed eagle (Zerbst).
The other side was similar except that the lettering in the centre read MOTH/UND/AUS/DAUER. The shields were as follows:—
Upper fly yellow field with a red star (Sternberg).
Upper staff white field with red rose (Lippe).
Lower fly arms of Bernberg.
Lower staff arms of Anhalt.

After the defection of the German troops to the allies in 1813 new units were raised and took part in the 1814 campaign against Napoleon. It is known that Anhalt-Dessau had one flag, Lippe-Detmold Schaumburg-Lippe and Waldeck two flags (one line, one Landwehr). The 'Danzig' flag of 1812 was possessed but not carried on this campaign. Reuss also had one flag.

7 Lippe contingent flag, known as the 'Danzig' flag.

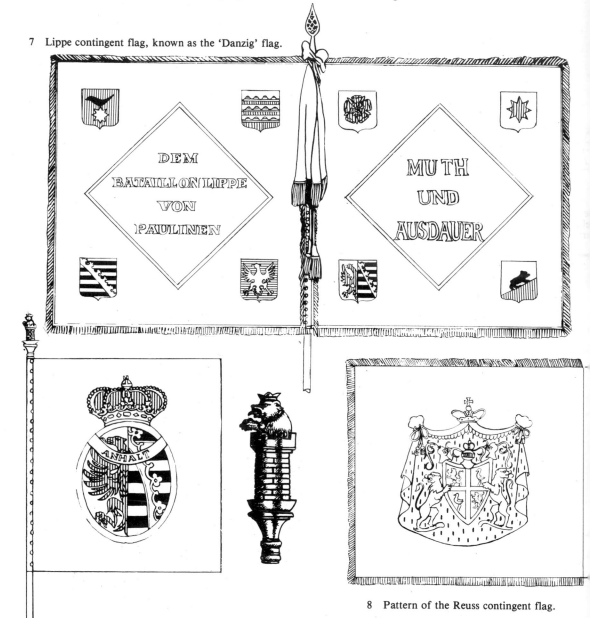

8 Pattern of the Reuss contingent flag.

6 Anhalt contingent flag 1811. The bear in the castle tower here shown on the flagstaff was originally the tip of the staff on an earlier vexellum type standard (the chains for which were held in the bears extended paw). According to some authorities this was used on the new flag as illustrated but the 1807 pattern certainly had a plain spear tip.

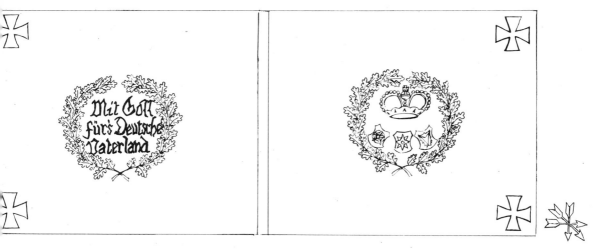

Flags of the combined Waldeck-Lippe, Schaumburg-Lippe battalions, 1814-1815. The two flags
[ar]e of similar design. That of the Landwehr unit was green and had crosses in the fly corners.
[Fie]lds were in their natural colours, all other decoration being in gold. The infantry flags had groups
[of a]rrows in place of the crosses and the colour of the flag may have been different, possibly white.

Baden

In 1806 the Baden infantry consisted of four regiments:— 1st 'Leibregiment', 2nd
'Erbgrossherzog', 3rd 'Markgraf Ludwig' and 4th 'von Harrant'. Each regiment
had two flags, a Leibfahne and a Bataillonsfahne, carried by senior NCOs.

In 1808 the infantry was reorganised, and this has caused some confusion
concerning regimental titles and distinctive colours. In 1809 the regiments were as
follows:—

No. 1 The Leibregiment.
No. 2 Grand Duke Hertitier.
No. 3 Markgraf Ludwig (formed from the 1st bttn. von Harrant and 2nd bttn.
Ludwig).
No. 4 von Harrant (formed from the 1st bttn. Ludwig and the 2nd bttn. von
Harrant).

The Leibregiment flag had a deep yellow field and red corner rays with gold
borders. The centre device on one side consisted of a gold 'CF' monogram
on a silver background surrounded by a green laurel wreath. The crown above
the monogram was gold with an ermine band. The wreath was tied top and
bottom with light blue ribbon. The corner devices were the 'CF' monogram
and crown in gold, the crown having the ermine band. The other side was similar
except that the central device was the shield of Baden (yellow with a red
diagonal) edged in gold and surrounded by a gold chain and red cross of the
order of Fidelity. Crown above the shield, and the corner devices, were as they
appeared on the opposite side. This description was made some years after the
end of the Napoleonic wars and the material had been replaced. It is probable
that the original material had had the same design as described for the other
regiments but in the colours red and yellow.

The other three regiments had flags of a common design. Each regiment had a distinctive colour:—

2nd regiment: Red

3rd regiment: Dark blue

4th regiment: Yellow

In all cases the field of the battalion flag was in the regimental colour with white corner rays, and the Leibflag was white with corner rays in the regimental colours. Design of both battalion and regimental flags was the same, with the devices in the same colours for both. Both sides of the flags were the same and the colours for the device were as follows:— Centre laurel wreath green (gold for fourth regiment) with gold crown and ribbon. Area within wreath yellow with red diagonal. Corner wreaths green (gold for fourth regiment) with gold crown, ribbon and 'CF' cypher. Grenades gold. Some authorities show the corner devices pointing outwards as on the Leibregiment, others inwards. Flag staffs were brown with brass staff heads. After 1808 the Leibflags were not carried.

In the cavalry the Garde du Corps had a vexillum standard. This was of silver cloth with silver fringes, cords, ribbons, chains and staff head device. The staff itself was white. On the cloth a silver griffin held in one hand a sword and in the other the arms of Baden (yellow with red diagonal) on an oval shield. The griffin stood on a green base and was backed by a trophy of arms in natural colours.

The Baden hussar regiment had two standards, one belonging to the Baden-Baden contingent, the other to the Baden-Durlach contingent. The standard of the latter was deep rose pink with silver embroidery and fringes. The staff was brown and the pike top brass. In the centre of the silver embroidered design were two oval shields bearing the arms of Baden and Bavaria. The arms of Baden were:—

The field divided into nine

1—Red with white checks.

2—Divided horizontally, white upper, yellow lower; the upper charged with a red rose, the lower with a black boar on a green base.

3—White with a red lion rampant.

4—Red, white vertical bar bearing three black chevrons.

9 Design described for the Leibregiment but probably spurious.

5—Yellow with red diagonal.

6—Blue charged with a white flag.

7—Yellow, top half of red lion rampant above blue wavy lines.

8—Divided vertically, left half yellow with red horizontal bar, right half yellow with blue lion rampant.

9—Blue and yellow checks.

The arms of Bavaria were quarterly, 1 and 4 blue and white lozenges, 2 and 3 black with yellow lion rampant.

The standard of the Baden-Baden contingent was white. The arms of Baden-Baden were borne on an oval shield in the centre in their proper colours as described for the Baden-Durlach standard. The shield was surrounded by a yellow ochre, ermine-lined mantle, and was supported by a silver griffin on the left and a silver twin-tailed lion on the right. A gold chain and order surrounded the shield and the whole design was supported on a silver scrollwork. The crown was silver with a red lining and silver ribbons tied the corners of the mantle. The decorative designs in the corners were in gold. Fringes were silver. Staff was deep yellow and was tipped with a gilt pike head. Some authorities state that these two standards were not carried during the Napoleonic Wars.

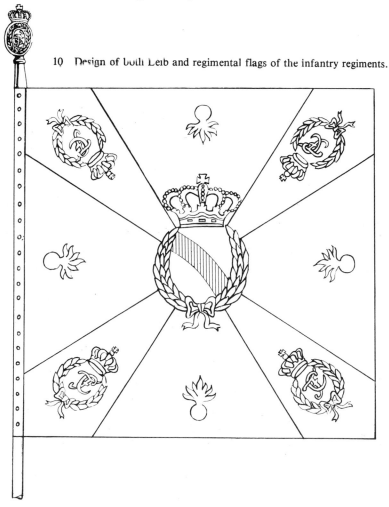

10 Design of both Leib and regimental flags of the infantry regiments.

11 Garde du Corps standard. Design and cloth were heavily embroidered.

12 Baden-Durlach contingent standard.

13 Baden-Baden contingent standard.

Bavaria

Many different patterns of flags were carried by the Bavarian armies during the Napoleonic wars. Confusion is caused by the appearance of new patterns, the retention and re-issue of old patterns and the individual interpretation of the regulations in the different regiments.

In 1786, flags of 173cm. square were issued. The Leibfahne was as per the illustration and was basically similar to the pre-1786 pattern. On the reverse side was the crest of Pfalz-Bayern with lion rampant supporters and below them the chains and orders of St. Hubert, the Lion of the Palatinate, and St. George. The crest at this time was (left to right, top to bottom): Cleve, red with gold wheel; Julich, gold a black lion rampant; Berg, silver a red lion rampant; Mors, gold a black horizontal bar. In the centre were the quartered arms of the Electorate of Bavaria; 1 and 4 diagonal lozenges of blue and white, 2 and 3 black a gold lion rampant; in the centre a red circle bearing a gold orb. Next came Bergen Op Zoom, red with three gold saltares above three green hills; Mark, checky red and silver; Veldenz, silver a blue lion rampant; Sponheim, three vertical rows of red and silver dicing; Ravensburg, silver with three red chevrons. Added in 1799 were the arms of Rappoltstein, silver with three black crowned ravens heads. The border was as for the other side.

The 1786 Regimentsfahne bore the same coat of arms as described above but on both sides, and on a blue central area within the same border as the Leibfahne. At this time one Leibfahne and one Regimentsfahne were carried per regiment. In 1801, two Leib- and two Regimentsfahne were carried, and in 1803 this was again changed to one Leib- and three Regimentsfahne. In 1804, this once more reverted to one Leib- and one Regimentsfahne. The Leibfahne was to be carried by the first battalion, the other by the second, and this was the regulation for the remainder of the Napoleonic wars.

The design of the Regimentsfahne was changed sometime before 1803, the arms of Bavaria only being used in place of the full coat previously described. These arms were borne on laurel and palm branches and had lion supporters. The whole design was on a blue background with the blue and white lozenge border (the number of rows in this border was normally three but two and four rows were used by some units). In 1803, the overall lozenge flag was introduced, the rows sometimes vertical, sometimes horizontal. This pattern was also reissued in 1813. New non-Catholic territories obtained in 1803 caused the discontinuation of the Virgin figure on the Leibfahnen, this being replaced by the Bavarian arms (quartered lions and lozenges). The crest has a rampant lion supporter and was contained within a mantle topped by an electiorial cap. The whole design was on a white field within the usual border. Many variations on the theme existed.

Throughout the period the flag staffs were tipped with gold spear-heads pierced or engraved with the following initials:—
1777-1799 Elector Carl Theodor, initial—CT
1799-1806 Elector Maximilian Joseph, initial—MJ

1806-1815 King Maximilian Joseph, initial—MJK

It was common practice to have a section (or even all) of the flag staff covered in blue corduroy. Various types of cravat were carried, some blue and white, some white with varying amounts of gold embroidery in various patterns and inscriptions.

The electorial cap on the 1807 flags was replaced by a crown in 1806, and in 1808 the crest was simplified to an overall lozenge pattern with a central red shield bearing an orb over crossed sceptre and sword in gold. This shield had two supporters and was shown on an ermine mantle. The whole design was on a blue background within the lozenge border on Regimentsfahnen, and on a white background often without a border on Leibfahnen. Both sides were the same. These flags were also issued in 1813 to those units that had lost their flags in Russia, and their staffs were covered in black leather.

In 1803 the cavalry carried one white (Leibstandarte) and two squadron (Eskadrons standarten) standards per division (two squadrons). Later the same year this was reduced to one Leib and one squadron standard per regiment, and in 1804 to one Leibstandarte per regiment. Only heavy cavalry (Dragoons and Kurassiers, etc.) carried standards. These standards bore on one side the quartered arms of Bavaria and on the other the double-headed eagle of the Holy Roman Empire. In 1814 the newly raised Garde du Corps and two Kurassier

14   1786 Leibfahne. Virgin in proper colours with blue gown over red undergarment. Globe blue, clouds white/grey. Stars and halo of the infant yellow. Scroll white with yellow lettering. Background to centre white with blue and white border.

regiments received new standards. (One Leib and two divisional per regiment). These standards measured between 40-45cm. square. The design was basically the same with the coat of arms as per the 1808 infantry standard on one side and the MJK monogram on the other. The Leib standards were white with gold embroidery and fringes, and the squadron standards were light blue, the second division having silver, and the third gold, embroidery. The Garde du Corps standards differed slightly in having a border of oak leaves rather than the edging of the other regiments. In the Kurassier regiments the central medallions were silver with gold letters and border on the Leibstandard and in the reverse colours for the divisional standards. The staffs were light blue and had similar tips to the infantry flags, cords and tassels were in gold. Cravats were blue and white with silver fringes.

15   Pattern for both Leib and regimental flags in 1803. The only difference between the two types was that the central area background was white on Leib and blue on regimental flags. All other colours were common to both types. Brown lion, silver crown with red lining and cushion. Red mantle with ermine lining and edging. Sword silver with gold hilt. Coat of arms: one and four, blue and white lozenges, two and three black with gold lions. Red central badge with gold orb. Frame to shield and mantle cords gold. Gilt spear head.

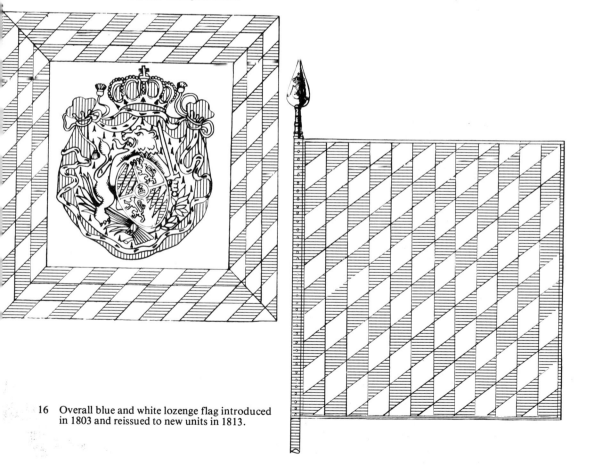

16   Overall blue and white lozenge flag introduced in 1803 and reissued to new units in 1813.

15

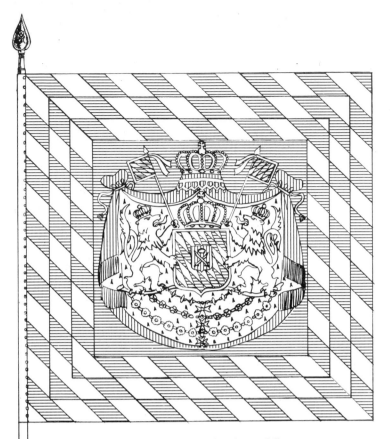

17 1808 pattern for both Leib and regimental flags.

18 and 19 These two drawings show the two sides of the 1814 pattern standards. No. 18 shows th[e] Garde du Corps oak leaf border and No. 19 the Kurassier regiments' pattern border.

Berg

During the period of Murat's reign over the Duchy of Berg both cavalry and infantry carried a colour of similar design. This was as shown in the illustration, the background colour being red with a white centre area. The coat of arms in the centre was in its proper colours which were as follows:— red mantle with gold edging and ermine lining. Gold crown with red lining and gold chain with white cross. Blue crossed batons with gold tips and eagles. Shield, right half red with gold emblem, left half white with red lion rampant crowned gold. Black anchor. Small escutcheon blue with gold eagle. The hanger for the order on the chain was in the form of a small blue heater shaped shield with the gold letter 'N' in the centre. The scroll above the arms was white with the motto DIEU LA GLOIRE ET LES DAMES. The infantry lost their colours in Spain. In 1809 when the Duchy came under the direct rule of Napoleon (in the capacity of regent for his nephew Louis) new colours were issued. These were as per the illustration and were white in colour. All emblems were in gold. The number in the top corner was the number of the regiment, that in the bottom corner the number of the battalion. The green guidon often attributed to the Chevaux-Legers Lanciers, bearing a grenade and the letters B and G in silver, was in fact a fanion of the Italian Foot Grenadiers of the Royal Guard. It seems that all flags and standards belonging to the Berg regiments were lost to the Russians at the crossing of the Beresina in 1812.

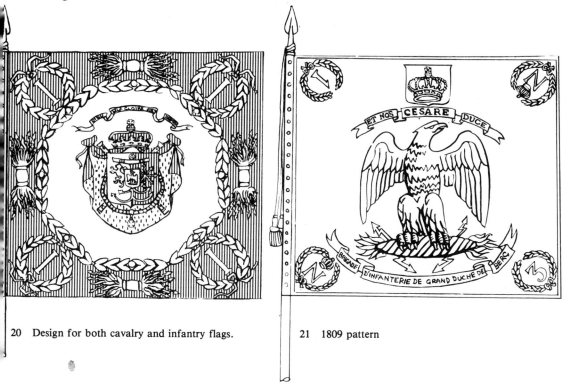

20 Design for both cavalry and infantry flags.

21 1809 pattern

Britain

The flags and standards of the British army during the Napoleonic period were, as now, of individual regimental design. All line infantry regiments had two flags per battalion, each carried by an ensign. One was the King's colour, which was an overall Union with the regimental badge in the centre. The other flag was the regimental which was usually in the regimental facing colour with the same badges as on the King's colour, and a small Union in the upper staff corner. Cords and tassels for all were gold and crimson mixed. Exceptions to this rule were regiments with red, black, or white facings, these colours being thought unsuitable for the flags. In the case of red and white facings the flag was white with a red (St. George's) cross, the Union and badges being over this in the same positions as for other regiments. Regiments with black facings were similar except that the red cross was on a black instead of a white background. The rules, such as they were, governing the design of flags and standards were contained in the 1768 warrant. It was here decreed that the infantry colours should measure 6 foot 6 inches by 6 foot on the pike. The pike was to be 9 foot 10 inches long including the ferrule and gilt spear head (6 inches). Devices could be either painted or embroidered onto the silk of the flag. The regulations concerning the design of regiments with black facings were also first stated in this warrant. The regimental badges were of many different patterns but in 1795 the shield design was introduced that became so widespread in use as to be almost regulation, except in Scottish regiments who rarely used it. In 1801 the union with Ireland caused the need for the addition of the cross saltire of St. Patrick to be added to the Union, and shamrocks to be added to the union wreath (until then entirely composed of roses and thistles) which surrounded the regimental badge on most colours. At this date those colours in good condition were altered to include the above changes but those in bad repair were laid up and new colours of the new pattern issued to their regiments.

In 1806 George Naylor, York Herald, was appointed inspector of regimental colours in an attempt to maintain some measure of control over the designs used. Naylor sent out a circular to discover details of colours used by all regiments in the army. The returns showed that most regiments were using the shield and that most were painted. Battle honours had been added to infantry flags since the word 'Gibraltar' was awarded to the 12th, 39th, 56th and 58th regiments, to be carried on their 2nd (regimental) colour, in 1784.

The footguard regiments had an entirely different system to the line. Although they only carried two colours at any one time during the period we are dealing with, each regiment had three 'King's' colours (previously the Colonel's, Lieutenant-Colonel's and Major's colours) and a regimental colour (Captain's colour) for each company. The Colonel's colour became the King's colour of the first battalion, the Lieutenant-Colonel's the second battalion and the Major's the third. Which of the regimental colours was to be carried at anyone time was worked on a set rotation basis. Each time it was necessary to issue new

regimental colours the next in line were used.

Colours and company badges of the First Foot Guards.

The Colonel's or 1st colour of the first battalion	Of crimson silk, bearing the imperial crown in the centre.
The Lieutenant-Colonel's, or 1st colour of the second battalion	Of crimson silk, bearing in the centre the Royal Cipher, reversed and interlaced, crown over. A small Union in the dexter canton.
The Major's or 1st colour of the third battalion	Of crimson silk, precisely similar to the Lieutenant-Colonel's colour except that a pile wavy, or ray, of gold issued from the corner of the small Union towards the centre.

The 2nd colours display the overall Union, and, in turn, bear the different company badges in the centre under an imperial crown, as follows:—

No. 1 company: A lion statant guardant gold, upon the imperial crown gold.
No. 2 company: A red and white rose (the Tudor rose).
No. 3 company: A gold fleur-de-lys.
No. 4 company: A gold portcullis.
No. 5 company: White rose, in a gold sun in glory.
No. 6 company: The thistle of Scotland proper.
No. 7 company: A gold harp.
No. 8 company: A red dragon on a green mound.
No. 9 company: White greyhound with a gold collar, on a green mound.
No. 10 company: Sun in splendour, a human face in the centre.
No. 11 company: A white unicorn gorged with a gold coronet and chain, on a green mound.
No. 12 company: White antelope, gorged with gold coronet and chain, on a green mound.
No. 13 company: White hart, gorged with a gold coronet and chain, resting on a green mound.
No. 14 company: A white falcon, wings extended on the barrel of a gold fetterlock.
No. 15 company: A red rose slipped and leaved.
No. 16 company: White swan, gorged with coronet and chain, on a green mound.
No. 17 company: White falcon, crowned and carrying a sceptre in the right talon, standing on the eradicated stump of a tree, from the left side of which issues a branch with three roses (one white between two red).
No. 18 company: Stump of a tree, with three leaves issuing from each side.
No. 19 company: A sceptre and a sword crossed saltire wise.
No. 20 company: Green oak tree with the crowned head of Charles II emerging from the centre of the foliage.
No. 21 company: Sun issuing from clouds.
No. 22 company: Beacon or cresset with flames.
No. 23 company: Two ostrich feathers crossed saltire wise.
No. 24 company: White hart issuing from a castle gateway on a heraldic wreath.

Colours and company badges of the Coldstream regiment of Foot Guards.

The Colonel's or 1st colour of the first battalion	Of crimson silk, bearing the star of the Order of the Garter, with the crown over.
The Lieutenant-Colonel's, or 1st colour of the second battalion	Of crimson silk, small Union in the dexter canton. In the centre a silver star of eight points within the Garter, crown over.
The Major's or 1st colour of the third battalion	As the Colonel's, with the addition of a small Union in the dexter canton, with a pile wavy issuing from the corner toward the centre.

The 2nd colours display the Union overall and in turn bear the different company badges in the centre, under an imperial crown, as follows:—

No. 1 company: A white lion statant on a green mound.
No. 2 company: The Prince of Wales' feathers and coronet.
No. 3 company: A white panther passant, spotted with various colours, flames of fire issuing from his mouth and ears, on a green mound.
No. 4 company: Two silver swords in saltire with gold hilts.
No. 5 company: St. George and the dragon.

No. 6 company: Red rose, seeded green, within the garter.

No. 7 company: A centaur on a green mound.

No. 8 company: Two sceptres in saltire, gold.

No. 9 company: The knot of the collar of the Garter Order, in gold, within the garter.

No. 10 company: A gold escarbuncle.

No. 11 company: A white boar passant, bristled gold, on a green mound.

No. 12 company: A dun cow on a green mound.

No. 13 company: A red and white rose impaled with a gold pomegranate with green stalk and leaves.

No. 14 company: A white galloping horse on a green mound.

No. 15 company: The crown of Charlemagne in gold.

No. 16 company: As No. 14 company.

Colours and company badges of the Scots Guards.

The Colonel's or 1st colour of the first battalion	Of crimson silk, in the centre the Royal Arms of Scotland; gold, a lion rampant within a double tressure flory counter flory red. Borne on an ordinary heraldic shield with a crown above and the motto 'En ferus hostis' below.
The Lieutenant-Colonel's or 1st colour of the second battalion	Of crimson silk, with a small Union in the dexter canton. In the centre the Union badge; rose, thistle and shamrock conjoined on one stalk. Crown above and motto 'Unita fortior' below.
The Major's or 1st colour of the third battalion	As that of the Lieutenant-Colonel with the addition of a small flame or pile wavy in gold, issuing from the lower corner of the Union. In the centre the star of the Order of the Thistle, with a crown above. Motto 'Nemo me impune lacessit'.

The second colours display the overall Union and each in turn bears one of the different company badges with crown above and motto below. These were as follows:—

No. 1 company: A red lion sejant affrontee on a silver shield. Motto 'In defence'.

No. 2 company: Bomb with lighted fuse. Motto 'Terrorem affero'.

No. 3 company: A red lion rampant. Motto 'Intrepidus'.

No. 4 company: Cross and figure of St. Andrew on a silver star. Motto 'Nemo me impune lacessit'.

No. 5 company: Red lion passant on gold shield. Motto 'Timere nescius'.

No. 6 company: Blue griffin on a gold shield. Motto 'Belloque ferox'.

No. 7 company: A salamander. Motto 'Per funera vitam'.

No. 8 company: A thunderbolt winged, and lightning. Motto 'Horror ubique'.

No. 9 company: A cannon firing. Motto 'Concusse cadent urbes'.

No. 10 company: A lizard. Motto 'Pascua nota mihi'.

No. 11 company: St. Andrew's cross on a shield. Motto 'Honores praefero'.

No. 12 company: A group of trophies of war. Motto 'Intaminata fides'.

No. 13 company: A spaniel dog. Motto 'Intaminata fides'.

No. 14 company: A red lion rampant. Motto 'Intrepidus'.

No. 15 company: A bomb with fuse. Motto 'Terrorem affero'.

As the King's colours were crimson and the regimental colours were the overall Union in each case, the guards regiments were in a way opposite to the line infantry.

In the cavalry, standards and guidons did not share the importance that the infantry colours enjoyed. Although carried by at least some regiments of cavalry during the earlier part of the Napoleonic wars, after 1812 standards and guidons were rarely, if ever, carried on campaign. According to the 1786 warrant the 'Regiments of Horse' were to have square standards (later the regiments of the Household Cavalry carried square standards) of silk damask; the regiments of Dragoon Guards, standards and guidons of silk damask; Dragoon and Light Dragoon regiments guidons of silk. The sizes were:—

Standards—2 feet 5 inches by 2 feet 3 inches deep (without fringes).
Guidons—3 feet 5 inches to end of slit by 2 feet 3 inches deep.
The guidons of the Light Dragoons were slightly smaller and were carried on shorter lances than those of other regiments which were 9 feet long. A Light Dragoon guidon of 1760 measured 2 feet 10 inches overall by 2 feet 4 inches deep.
The number of guidons carried varied with the number of troops in a regiment. In 1807, those regiments with a ten troop establishment had five guidons, those with twelve troops six. The first standard or guidon was the King's colour and was crimson with the Union badge. The second and subsequent standards or guidons were in the facing colour and bore the rank of the regiment, unless they were entitled to a badge of regimental distinction. Hussars did not carry standards or guidons.
Some of the individual badges as per the 1768 warrant were as follows:—

1st (King's) Dragoon Guards: King's cypher within garter.
1st (Royal) Dragoons: Arms of England within garter.
2nd (Royal North British) Dragoons, The Scots Greys: Thistle within circle of St. Andrew.
3rd (King's Own) Dragoons: White horse within garter.

22 Regimental colour 1st foot (Royals) 1790. These colours were probably retired soon after the union in 1801. Blue silk, red centre surrounded by green garter. Word 'Royal' on red oval edged in yellow. Union wreath and corner thistles in natural colours as was the crown. All lettering in yellow silk. King's colour carried the same designs without the corner thistles. In 1815 the colours bore no wreath nor 'Royal badge'. Central device similar to that shown. Corner badges upright and contained within crowned garters. Scroll above central device bore '1st or ROYALS'. Lettering 'THIRD BATT' below union. Below central device scroll with 'PENINSULAR' thereon and below that the sphinx badge.

5th (Royal Irish) Dragoons:	Crowned harp.
6th (Inniskilling) Dragoons:	Castle of Inniskilling.
3rd (Prince of Wales's) Dragoon Guards:	Three feathers issuing from coronet. Rising sun and red dragon badges in corners.
12th (Prince of Wales's) Light Dragoons:	Three feathers issuing from coronet. Rising sun and red dragon badges in corners.

There is little information on the flags carried by foreign units within the British army. It is known that the flags, standards and guidons of the King's German Legion followed the general design of their British counterparts. The infantry colours were the same size as the British, and there was one regimental and one King's colour per battalion. The cavalry had one King's standard plus a guidon for the second and subsequent squadrons. Prior to 1812 the cavalry was divided into Heavy and Light Dragoons. In 1812 the Light Dragoons became Hussars and the Heavy Dragoons became Light Dragoons. The Hussars would not have carried standards or guidons but it is likely that the new Light Dragoons used the same standards that were carried when they were Heavy Dragoons.

23   Regimental colour 42nd Highlanders 1802. Blue silk, red centre surrounded by blue garter. Crown, union wreath, St. Andrews badge, Sphinx and laurels embroidered in natural colours. Word 'Egypt' on yellow scroll. Regimental designation and border were in yellow silk as were the cyphers. King's colour carried the same devices but without corner cyphers. A second set of flags for this regiment of the same date and probably belonging to the second battalion were similar in design. Slight differences include the different pattern of cypher as shown here. The St. Andrew's badge was positioned on top of the confluence points of the wreath, with the top touching the end of the belt (which was buckled on the other side to that illustrated, and crossed in front of, rather than behind, at the cross over). The bottom of the St. Andrew's badge touched the top of the Egypt scroll. The regimental designation was placed horizontally on the union thus:— "XLII.Regt".

The colour of one other foreign unit, De Rolls regiment, dating from 1805, is illustrated. This regiment was in Egypt in 1800 and thus they were entitled to the sphinx badge. The King's would consist of an overall Union and probably bore the eye within a garter at its centre.

36 Central devices. (a) 28th foot, 1795. Red shield, gold lettering carried within union wreath like that shown in fig. 22. (b) 9th foot, 1799. Red silk with yellow scroll border. Figure of Britannia embroidered in natural colours. Unit designation in gold. Contained within an unusually thick wreath. (c) King's colour, 90th regiment, 1801. Red with yellow scroll border and lettering. Union wreath as per fig. 22. These colours were unusual in that the sphinx badge (d) when awarded was displayed in all four corners of the King's colour and the three unoccupied corners of the regimental colour. (e) 92nd Highlanders, 1801 to 1807. (f) 57th foot, 1804. Red shield, yellow embroidery. Unusual in that the battalion number is shown on the central device. Union wreath of the usual pattern. (g) King's and regimental colours the 52nd foot, 1807. Both of red silk with yellow borders. King's colour bore the crown and cypher in addition to the regimental number. Both central devices were within wreaths of the common pattern (as in fig. 32 etc). (h) 86th regiment, 1807, regimental colour. Red with gold border, crown and lettering. Crown has red lining, white pearls and ermine band. No wreath to this flag. (i) 27th foot, 1807. Colours similar to (n). Note wreath of laurels instead of the correct union wreath. (j) 10th regiment, 1808. Circle red with gold embroidery. White sphinx on blue oval with green laurels. All other items in proper colours. (k) 94th foot, 1812. In natural colours. King's colour had the same wreath but with a 'GR' cypher on a red circle in place of the crest, motto and supporters of the city of Edinburgh as on the regimental flag. (l) 57th regiment, 1813. Red with gold embroidery. Usual union wreath for this period (as per fig. 32 etc). (m) 92nd Highlanders, 1815 (Waterloo). Red disc, gold embroidery. Crown in natural colours. The King's and regimental colours carried the same devices. Usual wreath and sphinx badge below. Battle honours:— 'Peninsular' above the central device, 'Mandora' to the left and 'Egmont op Zee' to the right of the central device all on white scrolls. (n) 27th foot, 1815. Blue disc, white castle, gold lettering and border. Crown in natural colours. Usual union wreath with sphinx badge below. One battle honour 'Maida' above central device. The King's and regimental colours carried the same design. (o) Corner badges of 4th foot, 1815. This flag had as its central device the King's cypher within the crowned garter as per fig. 23. There was no wreath but in the three vacant corners of the regimental flag the lion badge in gold was shown. The regimental designation was carried on the horizontal arm of the St George's cross of the union in the canton in the following fashion:— 'IV or K.O.RL.RT'. The crowned central device only was carried on the King's colour.

24 Regimental colour De Rolls regiment 1805. Yellow silk. Inscription read:— 'Schwebe uber uns und segne unsere treue'.

25 King's colour, 78th Highlanders, 2nd battalion, 1805. Scrolls of blue silk. The traces of a circle visible around the elephant shows the area occupied by a previous design. Regimental designation on red silk oval with yellow border. On the regimental colour the designation was in one line along the horizontal bar of the union.

32 Regimental colour, 14th foot, 1812. Light yellow silk, red escutcheon with gold designation and border. Union wreath in natural colours, 'Corunna' in gold. As with all British colours, that part of the material attached to the staff was crimson. The 3rd battalion in 1815 had a similar flag but without 'Corunna' battle honour and with the shield bearing the inscription 'XIV REGT'.

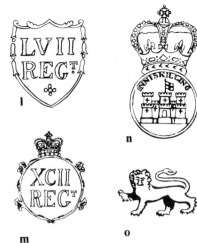

l

m

n

o

26 and 27 Regimental and King's colours of 3rd foot regiment 'the Buffs' 1807. Regimental colour yellow with green dragon. Blue scroll with gold edging Corner badges, crowns in natural colours over red roses on green stems. On both colours the regimental designation is in gold on a red oval bordered with gold.

37 King's guidon, 6th dragoons, 1801-15. Crimson silk. Union badge and crown in natural colours. Blue scroll, gold outline and lettering. Corner medallions yellow. Fringe and embroidery gold.

28 King's colour, 1st Foot Guards, 1815 (Waterloo), 3rd battalion. Crimson silk. Note the pile wavy, previously the distinction of the major's flag, by 1815 the mark of the 3rd battalion. The battle honour 'Barrosa' may have been carried below the monogram by 1815. All embroidery in gold.

29 Regimental colour, 1st Foot Guards, 1815 (Waterloo). Green dragon, crown in natural colours. Embroidery in gold.

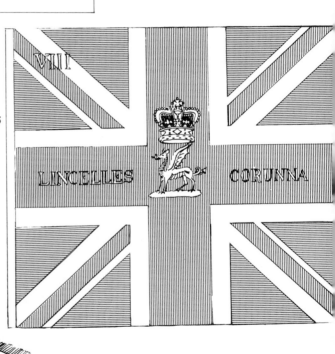

38 King's 1st guidon, 23rd Light Dragoons, 1803. Crimson, union badge and crown in usual colours. Gold embroidery and fringe. As the facings of this regiment were also crimson the other guidons were coloured blue for the difference.

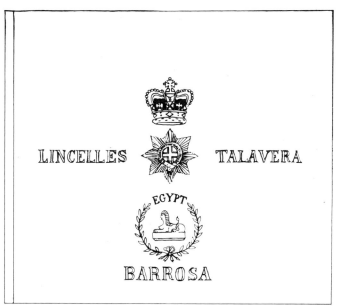

30 King's colour, 1st battalion Coldstream Guards, 1815 (Waterloo). Crimson with garter star and crown in proper colours. White sphinx within green laurels with word 'Egypt' in gold. Battle honours in gold. The 2nd battalion had a plain eight-point star in place of the garter star.

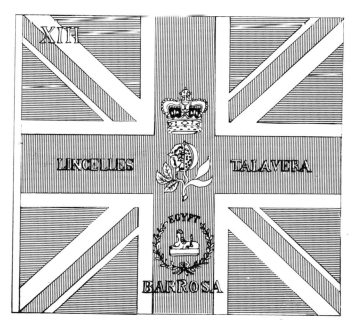

31 Regimental colour, Coldstream Guards, 1815 (Waterloo). The thirteenth company colour with rose and pomegranate badge under crown, all in proper colours. Battle honours and company designation in gold. These were carried by the second battalion at Waterloo.

33 Regimental colour, 33rd foot, 1815. Being a regiment bearing red facings the flag was white with red St. George cross. Union wreath natural colours, designation and border yellow. The King's colour bore the same central device.

34 Regimental colour, 23rd foot, 1815. Blue silk with white feathers and union in proper colours. Gold coronet and motto. Corner badges were a yellow sun rising over a green hill, a white horse on green ground with red background, a red dragon on a white ground. 'Egypt', sphinx and laurels in the usual colours. Battle honour on white scroll. King's colour had the same devices but without corner badges.

39 Regimental guidon, 2nd Heavy Dragoon, King's German Legion 1805-1812. Black with all devices in the usual colours. The 1st Regiment had blue guidons with an uncrowned wreath enclosing the inscription:— KING'S GERMAN DRAGOONS. At the confluence of the wreath stalks was a small red upright oval bearing the squadron number in gold.

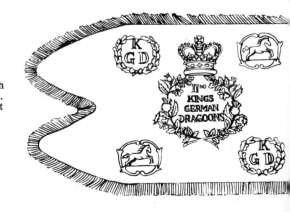

35 Regimental colour, 5th battalion King's German Legion, 1805-15. Blue silk, union wreath natural colours. All lettering and border to central area in gold. The central circle was the same colour as the background on both King's and regimental colours. The King's colour was similar to the regimental but the word 'PENINSULA' was absent, and there was a crown.

41 King's colour (standard), 1st Heavy Dragoons King's German Legion, 1805-12. Each regiment had a King's standard which was square and crimson plus one guidon per squadron in regimental facing colours. Union badge and crown were in natural colours. The white horses were on red backgrounds and the gold 'KGD' letters on blue backgrounds, all surrounded by gold embroidered borders. Fringes were gold.

40 King's Dragoon Guards, 1807-15. Blue with blue garter enclosing crimson centre on which the 'GR' cypher was displayed in gold. The backgrounds to the corner badges and the squadron number below the central device were crimson. The number 5 was gold and the laurels enclosing it light green. The union wreaths were in natural colours as was the crown. The horses were white, and all other embroidery and the fringes were gold.

42 King's standard, Life Guards, 1815. Crimson with union badge and crowns in natural colours. 'GR', 'PENINSULA' and fringe in gold. Motto scroll gold with black lettering.

Brunswick

It is not known what flags, if any, were carried by the Brunswick Black Corps before 1814. At Waterloo the three line battalions carried two flags each, the Herzogsfahne (Duke's flag) and the Bataillonsfahne (Regimental flag). The Light battalions, Leib battalion (which had been raised as a light battalion), the avant guard and regiments of cavalry did not carry colours. The flags of the three line battalions were as follows:—

1st battalion. Both Duke's and regimental flags had a gilt spear point to the 300cm.-long staff. The design on the spearpoint was the Duke's monogram above the leaping horse of Hanover. Cords and tassels were yellow and silver mixed.

The Herzogsfahne bore on the one side three horizontal bands, coloured from the top to the bottom yellow, light blue, yellow. In the centre of the light blue band were the Ducal arms. These consisted of a red, ermine-lined mantle tied at the corners with gold cords. The crown above this was gold with an ermine band, red interior and pearl on the arches. The shield bore, reading from the top left, blue lion rampant on a gold field with a semy of red hearts, red with two gold lions passant, blue with a white rampant lion armed and crowned red, a blue and white border, a red field with gold lion rampant, gold with red lion rampant armed and crowned blue, red with gold lion rampant armed blue, white with two bear's claws in black in chief, below which was a white band with red lines on top and bottom edges and in the centre, below which there were two rows of blue and white checks, red and silver horse, three rows of red and silver checks in chief below which a yellow field bore two red lines, silver with a red antler, silver with a black stag, silver with a black antler. The corner devices were silver. On the other side the flag was yellow with a broad, light blue cross. All the decorations were in silver. The flag had silver fringes on three sides.

The Bataillonsfahne was probably of a similar size to the Herzogsfahne. It bore on one side, on a yellow field, a large light blue centre lozenge, similar to the French 1804 pattern. In the centre of this lozenge were the Ducal arms. It is probable that in each yellow corner the Duke's crowned monogram was displayed (without wreath). The other side had the same background with all decorations in silver. The flag was silver fringed.

2nd battalion. The Herzogsfahne was 140cm. square and had a crowned disc as its staff top. Cords and tassels were silver and yellow mixed. The field was divided into horizontal bands coloured, from top to bottom, light blue, yellow, light blue. In the centre of the yellow band was a black rectangle. On this black rectangle was a wreath of laurel and palm in white; within the wreath was a red ground, and upon this a white horse. On the other side was a black lozenge in the same position as the black rectangle. The centre of the lozenge bore in five lines the words:—

MIT/GOTT/FÜR FURST UND/VATERLAND/1813

In the two corners above the lozenge were crowns and, in the corners below, monograms.

The Bataillonsfahne was also 140cm. square and consisted of three bands coloured from top to bottom, light blue, black, light blue on both sides. On one side the centre black band bore in the middle a crowned FW cypher within a laurel wreath all in silver. On the other side the black band bore the Ducal arms in proper colours within a silver wreath. Between the branches of the wreath above the coat of arms was the inscription:—

Ist Gott fur uns, wer mag wider uns seyn—also in silver.

3rd battalion. Herzogsfahne measured 144cm. by 150cm. long. Both sides were the same. The field was blue with all designs worked in silver embroidery.

The Bataillonsfahne was 142cm. square. The flag was black with a large central rectangle, on one side light blue, on the other yellow. On the light blue rectangle there was a silver horse with the motto:— NUNQUAM RESTRORSUM in a semi-circle above it. On the other side was a silver laurel wreath tied with a red ribbon. Within the wreath was the legend:— Mit Gott Fur Furst und Vaterland MDCCCXIV; above which was the Ducal crown. Below the knot tying the laurel, was a silver death's head. This flag had cords and tassels of mixed gold and yellow.

A slightly different version of this flag has also been recorded. This bore within the rectangles of both the blue and yellow sides, a white horse. Below this the inscription GOTT MIT US/ANNO/XVIXXI in three lines was shown. A wreath surrounded all the designs. It is possible that this was an earlier or later

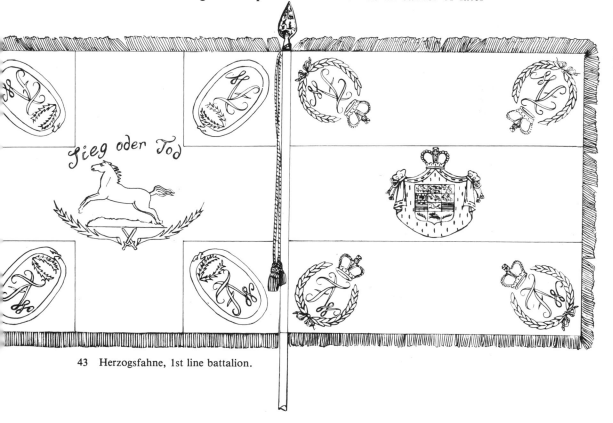

43   Herzogsfahne, 1st line battalion.

pattern, or simply incorrectly reported. Similarly, there is also reference to a yellow, light blue, yellow flag with crowned FW and laurel as for the Bataillonsfahne of the second battalion. It would seem logical that this would be a design for a first battalion flag, again of a later or earlier date to those shown, but there is no indication of ownership or explanation available. It is possible that these were designs made but not utilised.

44   Bataillonsfahne, 1st line battalion.

45   Herzogsfahne, 2nd line battalion.

46   Bataillonsfahne, 2nd line battalion.

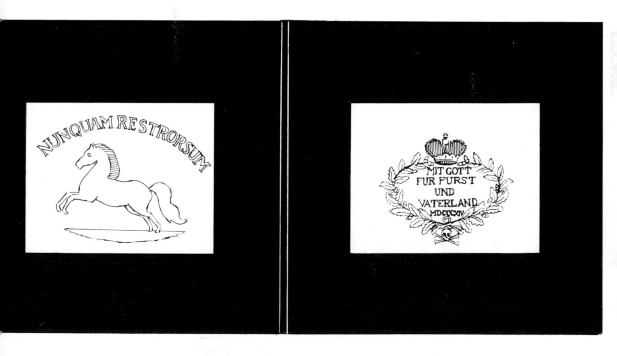

47   Herzogsfahne, 3rd line battalion.

Denmark

Infantry regiments in the Danish army by 1813 consisted of four battalions. The first and second battalions were made up of the original regular troops, and the third and fourth were raised from the disbanded militia units. The first battalion had one company of grenadiers and three of musketeers, the other battalions had one company of riflemen and three of musketeers each. The grenadiers and the third and fourth battalions each had two flags of national design (red with a white cross and gold cyphers within green wreaths in the corners) and these were the same for all regiments. The first battalion musketeers and the second battalions each had two flags of a regimental design (both the same). The field of the regimental colours was in the regimental facing colour, all other devices being common to all. The exact size is not known but they approximated 132cm. square. They were normally carried by a senior NCO, and all the devices were painted.

The hussars had two standards (one for each squadron) and were both of the same design. These were of crimson cloth and measured approximately 55cm. by 64cm. On one side there was a silver dove in the centre with a blue ribbon in its beak. The other side bore the King's monogram in the centre. The regiments of light dragoons had one standard for each squadron (supposedly four in number); they measured 55cm. by 64cm. and were carried by a senior NCO on a staff 250cm. long. All the standards were of the same design and, like the

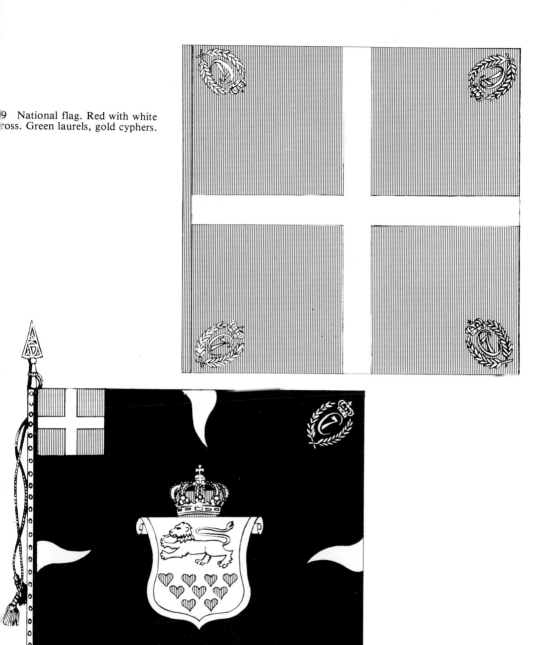

49 National flag. Red with white cross. Green laurels, gold cyphers.

50 Regimental flag, 3rd Jutland infantry regiment. Black (facing colour of regiment). Gold shield and crown. Red hearts and cushion to crown. Blue lion. Red canton with white cross. Green wreath with gold cyphers. White 'flames' (these varied in colour according to regiment).

infantry flags of the first and second battalions, bore the devices on a field of the regimental facing-colour.

The Royal Horseguard (Der Kongelige Livgarde til Hest) was composed of two squadrons. The standard of the first squadron had a background colour of light greyish blue and is shown in the illustration. The standard of the second squadron was known to have a background of red but no other details are known. However it is possible that the design was similar, with squadron distinctions being limited to the colour of the backgrounds.

51 Cavalry standard, Jutland Light dragoons. Dark green (facing colour of regiment). Red scroll with gold lettering. Gold crown, shield, central and corner wreaths, cyphers, 'flames' and roman numeral date. Red hearts and cushion to crown. Blue lion. Red canton with white cross. Gilt tip with gold cords and tassels. White strip under fixing studs.

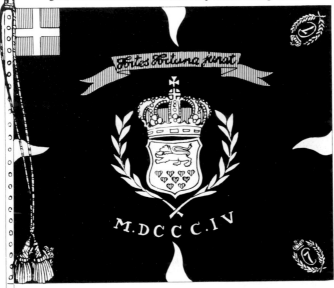

52 Standard of Royal Horseguards. Blue-grey field with white border outside the gold embroidered framework. Coat of arms as follows:— field divided into quarters by white cross. First quarter, blue lions on a yellow field. Second quarter, yellow beast on red field. Third quarter, in chief yellow crowns on blue field above blue lions on yellow field. Fourth quarter, in chief a blue lion and eight red hearts on a yellow field above a yellow dragon on a red field. Centre escutcheon, mainly red with yellow charges. Chain and crown gold, the latter with red lining. Supporters in natural colours standing on gold base.

France

The armies of the new Republic of France carried many flags of different patterns. Red, white and blue arranged in many different designs, and charged with various republican symbols and slogans were the common factors. In 1791, a tricolour flag (blue nearest the staff) was decreed. This bore in the centre the letters 'RF' or the words in full 'Republique Francaise', surrounded by a laurel wreath all in gold. In the corners reading from the centre was the number of the demi-brigade also in gold. A tricolour ribbon was attached at the pike-head. The facine was a popular symbol, and illustrations '53' and '54' show two patterns of 1796 bearing this design. The flag shown in '53' is of the fifth demi-brigade. The ground is white and the diamonds red and blue—those near the staff:- upper blue, lower red; those near the fly:- upper red, lower blue. The facine is brown bound with white tapes and the axe-heads silver. Oak leaves are green, and the cap is tricoloured from the top blue, white, red. All lettering and numbers are gold. The pike head is brass and a tricolour ribbon and cords are attached. The bodies of the tassels are tricoloured from the top blue, white, red. Illustration '54' shows the flag of the twelfth demi-brigade. The two triangles on the upper and lower edges are blue, those on the left and right sides being red. The diamond shapes forming the central portion of the design are red top and bottom, blue both sides. The areas between the coloured sections are white. The central devices are the same colours as described for '53'.

In 1797, some attempt at standardisation was made and the demi-brigades in Italy received new flags all of a similar basic design. These flags were 160cm. square and were the pattern carried by the French infantry in Egypt. This pattern was blue with a white centre panel on both sides. The small scalene triangles were red and the areas between these and the blue field were white. The centre panel on the obverse bore a brown facine bound and surrounded with green laurels. The axe heads were silver and the revolutionary cap red. On the reverse the centre panel bore a green laurel and often the demi-brigade number. Although all of the same basic design there were various regimental and battalion differences.

Each battalion had a flag, and the number in an abbreviated form was shown in the upper right hand corner on the side that bore the facine. This number was also shown in the lower left hand corner in some demi-brigades, with the two remaining corners having the demi-brigade number displayed in figures. The abbreviations for the battalions were as follows:-
PER BON or P.BON for the first battalion
DME BON for the second and
TME BON for the third. This lettering, as with all lettering on these flags, was usually in gold or white paint.

In some cases battle honours were added in paint to the white square above and around the revolutionary cap. More usually, battle honours were painted in white on the body of the flag on the reverse side. The demi-battalion number was often painted in the centre of the laurel wreath on this side. Flag staffs were topped by a brass pike head to which tricoloured cravats, cords and tassels were often attached. Staffs were usually painted black or in red, white and blue spirals. The bottom of the staff had a brass ferrule so that it could be dug into the ground and thus relieve the bearer of the weight.

53   5th Demi-Brigade, 1796.

54   12th Demi-Brigade, 1796.

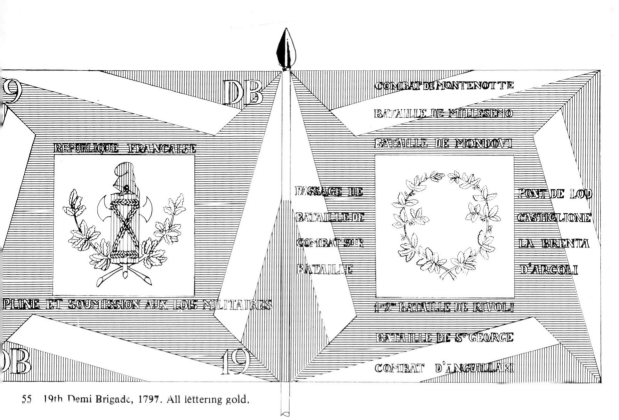

55 19th Demi Brigade, 1797. All lettering gold.

In 1804 the famous eagles were issued to regiments. The actual flag was now of only secondary importance, value having been transferred to the eagle. These eagles were 12 inches high from the top of the head to the bottom of the socket. Numerals in metal were attached to the plinth to indicate the regiment to which it belonged. Initially, each battalion received an eagle and this was carried by a sergeant major. The flag pattern was as shown in the illustration '56'. The centre sections were white, the corner triangles red and blue. The top staff and lower fly were blue on both sides, the lower staff and upper fly being red on both sides. All lettering and embellishments were gold. Staffs were blue. This flag measured 80cm. by 80cm. The design was general throughout the line infantry with only the number of regiment and battalion differing. Some special and foreign units had slightly different lettering and detail alterations. A few examples are given below:—

The 10th Demi-Brigade of Veterans carried a flag of the same general design as described above but the laurels bordering the central white square were divided by a rosette in the centre of each run, with the laurel leaves leaning towards the rosette on both half runs, rather than leaning all in one direction as on the usual design. The centre of the corner laurels were light blue rather than the base triangle colour and bore the number 10 in gold. The inscriptions read:—
L'EMPEREUR/DES FRANCAIS/A LA 10eme DEMI-BRIGADE/DE
VETERANS

and on the other side,

LE COURAGE/NE VIEILLIT PAS/ler BATTALION

This flag was carried from 1804-10.

The Swiss 3rd Demi-Brigade Helvetique had, in 1805, a flag of the general pattern with the following inscriptions:—

L'EMPEREUR/DES FRANCAIS/A LA 3e DEMI-BRIGADE/HELVETIQUE

and on the reserse,

VALEUR/ET DISCIPLINE

There was no number on the plinth of the eagle.

The flag of the Ecole Imperiale Militaire Saint Cyr, 1805-14 was of the usual pattern but, in common with other special units, there were no numbers in the corner wreaths nor on the plinth of the eagle. The inscriptions for this flag read:—

L'EMPEREUR/DES FRANCAIS/AUX ÉLÈVES/DE L'ÉCOLE IMPERIALE/MILITAIRE

and on the reverse,

ILS S'INSTRUISENT/POUR VAINCRE

In 1808 it was decreed that only one eagle was to be carried per regiment and that by the first battalion. The eagles and flags of the other battalions were to be returned to the regimental depots but it is to be expected that this took some time to be fully implemented and probably not completely complied with until 1811. In 1808 it was also decided that an ensign of long service should carry the eagle, to be supported by a properly selected colour guard of NCOs. Regiments often carried the eagle without the unimportant flag, sometimes on the bare staff, and sometimes with a tricoloured cravat replacing the flag. Gold wreaths were added to the eagles of regiments involved in the 1805 campaign in Germany. That of the 8th regiment was taken by the British 87th regiment at Barrosa. The wreath was fitted around the neck of the eagle resting on its shoulders and fixed with two screws.

The desire to add battle honours to the flags and standards of the French army necessitated the adoption of a new design. The vertical tricolour was decided upon in 1811 but not before many different designs had been suggested and rejected. These included a green flag with white central lozenges; a green flag with a white cross, golden bees on the green sections, and a gold crowned eagle in the centre of the cross; a flag of a different colour for each arm with a white central lozenge bearing on one side the imperial arms and on the other a blue globe similar to the flags described in the Italian section; a green flag with a white star decorated with various bees, laurels, and inscriptions, and a similar design in different colours for each arm; a red and blue quartered flag bearing a white cross, golden sun, crowned N, Legion d'Honneur and green laurels. It is interesting that many of the designs put forward used green as the base, this being Napoleon's favourite colour. Napoleon however had no wish to dispense with the red, white and blue, and the new flags and standards began to be issued at the beginning of 1812. The eagle remained exactly the same as before with

56 3rd regiment infantry of the line. 1804 pattern.

L'EMPEREUR DES FRANÇAIS, AU 3ᵉᵐᵉ REGIMENT D'INFANTERIE DE LIGNE

57 Westphalian regiment in French service, 1807-15. This measured 164cm square. Colours were the same as its French counterparts. The other side bore the inscription VALEUR/ET DISCIPLINE/Ier BATAILLON. This was the pattern used by most foreign units in the French army.

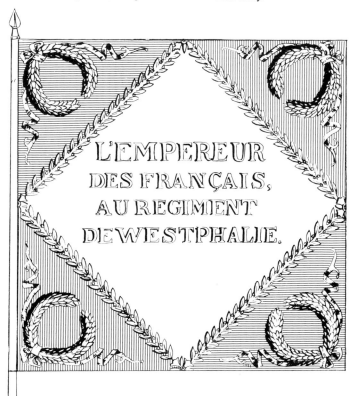

L'EMPEREUR DES FRANÇAIS, AU REGIMENT DE WESTPHALIE.

only the pattern of the flag changing. This was blue, white, red with blue always at the staff; all decorations and inscriptions were in gold. The inscriptions were the designation of the unit on one side with battle honours on the other. The following table shows the battle honours for each regiment:—

Regiments of the infantry of the line
1st regiment—WAGRAM
2nd regiment—ECKMUHL, ESSLING, WAGRAM.
3rd regiment—ULM, AUSTERLITZ, JENA, FRIEDLAND, ECKMUHL, ESSLING, WAGRAM.
4th regiment—ULM, AUSTERLITZ, JENA, EYLAU, ECKMUHL, ESSLING, WAGRAM.
5th regiment—WAGRAM.
8th regiment—AUSTERLITZ, JENA, FRIEDLAND, ESSLING, WAGRAM.
9th regiment—WAGRAM.
11th regiment—ULM, WAGRAM.
12th regiment—AUSTERLITZ, JENA, EYLAU, ECKMUHL, WAGRAM.
13th regiment—WAGRAM.
14th regiment—ULM, AUSTERLITZ, JENA, EYLAU.
15th regiment—FRIEDLAND.
16th regiment—ECKMUHL, ESSLING, WAGRAM.
17th regiment—AUSTERLITZ, JENA, EYLAU, ECKMUHL, ESSLING, WAGRAM.
19th regiment—WAGRAM.
21st regiment—AUSTERLITZ, JENA, EYLAU, WAGRAM.
23rd regiment—WAGRAM.
24th regiment—JENA, EYLAU, FREIDLAND, ESSLING, WAGRAM.
25th regiment—AUSTERLITZ, JENA, EYLAU, ECKMUHL, WAGRAM.
27th regiment—ULM, JENA, EYLAU, FRIEDLAND, ESSLING, WAGRAM.
28th regiment—WAGRAM.
30th regiment—AUSTERLITZ, JENA, EYLAU, ECKMUHL, WAGRAM.
32nd regiment—ULM, FRIEDLAND.
33rd regiment—AUSTERLITZ, JENA, EYLAU, ECKMUHL, WAGRAM.
34th regiment—ULM, AUSTERLITZ.
35th regiment—ULM, WAGRAM.
36th regiment—ULM, AUSTERLITZ, JENA, EYLAU.
37th regiment—ECKMUHL, ESSLING, WAGRAM.
39th regiment—ULM, JENA, EYLAU, FRIEDLAND, ESSLING, WAGRAM.
40th regiment—ULM, AUSTERLITZ, WAGRAM.
42nd regiment—WAGRAM.
43rd regiment—ULM, AUSTERLITZ, JENA, EYLAU.
44th regiment—JENA, EYLAU.
45th regiment—AUSTERLITZ, JENA, FRIEDLAND, ESSLING, WAGRAM.
46th regiment—ULM, AUSTERLITZ, JENA, EYLAU, ECKMUHL, WAGRAM.
50th regiment—ULM, JENA, EYLAU, FRIEDLAND.
51st regiment—AUSTERLITZ, JENA, EYLAU.
52nd regiment—WAGRAM.
53rd regiment—WAGRAM.
54th regiment—AUSTERLITZ, JENA, FRIEDLAND, ESSLING, WAGRAM.
55th regiment—ULM, AUSTERLITZ, ESSLING, EYLAU.
56th regiment—ECKMUHL, ESSLING, WAGRAM.
57th regiment—ULM, AUSTERLITZ, JENA, EYLAU, ECKMUHL, ESSLING, WAGRAM.
58th regiment—ULM, FRIEDLAND.
59th regiment—ULM, JENA, EYLAU, FRIEDLAND, ESSLING, WAGRAM.
60th regiment—WAGRAM.
61st regiment—AUSTERLITZ, JENA, EYLAU, ECKMUHL, WAGRAM.
62nd regiment—WAGRAM.
63rd regiment—JENA, EYLAU, FRIEDLAND, ESSLING, WAGRAM.
64th regiment—ULM, AUSTERLITZ, ESSLING, WAGRAM.
65th regiment—ECKMUHL.
67th regiment—ECKMUHL, ESSLING, WAGRAM.
69th regiment—ULM, JENA, EYLAU, FRIEDLAND, ESSLING, WAGRAM.
72nd regiment—FRIEDLAND, ECKMUHL, ESSLING, WAGRAM.
75th regiment—ULM, AUSTERLITZ, JENA, EYLAU.
76th regiment—ULM, JENA, EYLAU, FRIEDLAND, ESSLING, WAGRAM.
79th regiment—WAGRAM.
81st regiment—WAGRAM.

84th regiment—ULM, WAGRAM.
85th regiment—AUSTERLITZ, JENA, EYLAU, ECKMUHL, WAGRAM.
88th regiment—ULM, AUSTERLITZ, ESSLING, WAGRAM.
92nd regiment—ULM, WAGRAM.
93rd regiment—ECKMUHL, ESSLING, WAGRAM.
94th regiment—AUSTERLITZ, JENA, FRIEDLAND, ESSLING, WAGRAM.
95th regiment—AUSTERLITZ, JENA, FRIEDLAND, ESSLING, WAGRAM.
96th regiment—ULM, FRIEDLAND, ESSLING, WAGRAM.
100th regiment—ULM, ESSLING, WAGRAM.
102nd regiment—WAGRAM.
103rd regiment—ULM, ESSLING, WAGRAM.
105th regiment—JENA, EYLAU, ESSLING, WAGRAM.
106th regiment—WAGRAM.
108th regiment—AUSTERLITZ, JENA, EYLAU, ECKMUHL, WAGRAM.
111th regiment—AUSTERLITZ, JENA, EYLAU, ECKMUHL, WAGRAM.
112th regiment—WAGRAM.
The 31st, 38th, 41st, 49th, 68th, 71st, 73rd, 74th, 77th, 78th, 80th, 83rd, 87th, 89th, 90th, 91st, 97th, 98th, 99th, 104th, 107th, 109th and 110th were vacant numbers in the army list in 1812, the 104th and 107th being reformed in 1814.
The regiments 6th, 7th, 10th, 20th, 22nd, 47th, 66th, 70th, 82nd, 86th, and 101st of the line did not carry battle honours as they did not take part in any of these battles with the Grand Armee, being with the army in Italy, Spain, the Colonies or on other duties.
Battle honours for the light infantry were as follows:-
2nd regiment—FRIEDLAND.
3rd regiment—ECKMUHL, ESSLING, WAGRAM.
4th regiment—ULM, FRIEDLAND.
5th regiment—WAGRAM.
6th regiment—ULM, JENA, EYLAU, FRIEDLAND, ESSLING, WAGRAM.
7th regiment—JENA, EYLAU, ECKMUHL, WAGRAM.
8th regiment—WAGRAM.
9th regiment—ULM, FRIEDLAND, ESSLING, WAGRAM.
10th regiment—ULM, AUSTERLITZ, JENA, EYLAU, ECKMUHL, ESSLING, WAGRAM.
12th regiment—FRIEDLAND.
13th regiment—AUSTERLITZ, JENA, EYLAU, ECKMUHL, WAGRAM.
15th regiment—AUSTERLITZ, ECKMUHL, WAGRAM.
16th regiment—JENA, EYLAU, FRIEDLAND, ESSLING, WAGRAM.
18th regiment—ULM, WAGRAM.
21st regiment—ESSLING, WAGRAM.
23rd regiment—WAGRAM.
24th regiment—ULM, AUSTERLITZ, JENA, EYLAU, ECKMUHL, ESSLING, WAGRAM.
25th regiment—ULM, JENA, FRIEDLAND, ESSLING, WAGRAM.
26th regiment—ULM, AUSTERLITZ, JENA, EYLAU, ECKMUHL, ESSLING, WAGRAM.
27th regiment—AUSTERLITZ, JENA, FRIEDLAND, ESSLING, WAGRAM.
28th regiment—ESSLING, WAGRAM.
Numbers 11, 20, 29 and 30 were vacant. Regiments 1st, 14th, 19th, 22nd, 31st, 32nd had no battle honours.

During the defence of Paris in 1814 'La Garde Nationale' carried a flag of the 1812 pattern but with all embroidery and fringes in silver. The inscription read:—
GARDE/NATIONALE/DE/PARIS

Several regiments of volunteers were also raised in 1814. A flag of one such unit was a simple tricolour with a green wreath of oak and laurel in the centre column. Within the wreath were the inscriptions:—
CHALON/SUR/SAÔNE
and on the other side,
HONNEUR/ET/PATRIE

During the First Restoration of 1814 new flags were issued of a royal pattern. For the infantry of the line these measured 150cm. square, were white in colour and had a border of Fleurs-de-lis and roses in gold. Each corner bore the regimental number within a square. The centre device was on one side a wreath composed of laurels (for one arm of the wreath) and oak leaves (for the other arm). Hung from the stalks of the wreath were the orders of the Legion d'Honneur and St. Louis on red ribbons. Within the wreath was the inscription in gold and shadowed in black:—

LE ROI/AU REGIMENT/(Name of regiment)/(Number of regiment)/d'INFANTRY/DE LIGNE

The other side was similar with the inscriptions in the centre of the laurels replaced by the Royal Arms of France. Cravats were white with a gold Fleurs-de-lis border near the ends, and a gold fringe. On Napoleon's return from Elba in 1815 the regiments of the line received new flags and eagles. The eagle was the same design as carried since 1804 but of cheaper manufacture. The flag was of a much more simple design than those previously carried. It consisted of a simple tricolour (blue nearest the staff) with only a narrow fringe and light embroidery around the edges. Cravat was tricoloured and had gold embroidery and fringes. Inscriptions were as shown in the illustration, and most regiments carried the same battle honours as shown in the list for 1812. One known exception to this was the flag for the 85th regiment of line which had the battle honour 'ULM' added to those borne in 1812.

During the period 1804-15 the eagles for the regiments of the Guard were exactly the same as those of the line, and the flags were also of the same general design. Prior to this date the Guard had flags of individual design. Illustrated is the flag of the Foot Grenadiers of the Consular Guard 1800-1804. This measured 176cm. and was carried on a 336cm. long blue velvet-covered staff. The staff was bound with gold wire and the pike-head was gilt. The centre diamond and the border of the flag were white. The embroidery and outline to the border were gold. The four triangles formed between the centre diamond and the border were:— blue, the two nearest the staff; and red, the two nearest the fly. All were covered in a semee of golden grenades. The central sunburst was gold with the letters R.F. in silver. Fascines and branches to the laurel and oak sprigs were brown, with all leaves green, including those binding the fascines. Spear heads were silver. The scroll above the sun was white with a gold outline and lettering. Cords and tassels were gold and the embroidery and fringe on the tricolour cravat was also gold. The light infantry had a similar flag but the background to the border was green and the grenades on the red sections and fascines were replaced by hunting horns (a single horn replacing both fascines). The 1804 pattern flag for the Guard infantry regiments differed from those of the line in that the corner wreaths enclosed symbols relevant to the regiment i.e. grenades for grenadier regiments, hunting horns for chasseurs, anchors for marines etc. Some had a badge incorporating the imperial eagle on one side as illustrated for the marines. All decorations were gold. The flag of the Velites de Turin of the Imperial Guard in 1810, bore grenades in the corner wreaths and the inscriptions as follows:—

Obverse, L'EMPEREUR/DES FRANCAIS/AU BLON DE VELITES/DE TURIN

6th Light Infantry, 1812. Standard pattern for all line regiments at this time.

and on the reverse, GARDE/IMPERIALE/VALEUR/ET DISCIPLINE.
There was no eagle the staff having a plain pike head, this unit not having an eagle as Velites, being attached to other units as third battalions, owed their allegiance to the eagle of the parent unit. With the additions of further regiments to the guard in 1811 it was necessary to modify the flags so as to indicate the number of the regiment. The corner wreaths now carried the number of the regiment, as in the line where there was more than one regiment of a particular type e.g. grenadiers. The inscription also changed and in most cases the eagle badge disappeared. The flag for the first grenadiers is illustrated, and this was the general pattern for the majority of units. All colours were the same as previous patterns. The reduction in the number of eagles that took place in 1811 affected the guard in the same way that it affected the line infantry. For the campaign in 1812 only one eagle was to be carried by each arm, and by the first regiment in each case.

The change to the tricolour in 1812 for the line regiments did not happen for the guards until 1813. As before, one flag was issued to each regiment to be carried by the first battalion. These were exactly the same as for the line except that the upper and lower wreaths contained a badge for the arm. Illustrated is the flag for the second grenadiers. The plinth of the eagle bore the words 'Garde Imperiale'. All flag staffs were, as for the line, painted blue. During Napoleon's exile on Elba he was attended by a small force of his guard. This force was known as the Battalion Napoleon and was permitted to carry the flag illustrated. This was 80cm. square and was white. The diagonal bands were crimson with gold crowned 'N' and bees. The lettering was crimson. The staff was painted in crimson and white diagonals, and surmounted by a gilt pike head. The cravat was crimson and white and had embroidery in gold. Cords, tassels and fringes to flag and cravat were gold.

In 1815 the Guard was issued with new flags. Only one example of a Guard flag for this period is known and that is for the horse artillery. If it can be assumed that this was the pattern for all Guard units then the flag was of the 1812 design. 'N's appeared in all wreaths and no designation of unit was shown, but instead a list of cities as follows:—
VIENNE/BERLIN, MADRID/MILAN, MOSCOU/WARSOVIU/VENISE/LE CLAIRE
on the reverse the battle honours:—
MARENGO, ULM/AUSTERLITZ, JENA/EYLAU, FRIEDLAND/WAGRAM/LA MOSKOWA/LUTZEN, MONTMIRAIL.
The 'Garde Nationale' in 1815 had flags similar to those carried in 1814. One belonging to the 'Garde Nationale De L'Ile d'Elbe' was taken by the Prussians on their entry to Paris. This flag was of the 1812 pattern but all embroidery and fringes were in silver. The inscriptions were as follows:—
L'EMPEREUR/NAPOLEON/A LA GARDE/NATIONALE/DE L'ILE D'ELBE
and on the other side:— CHAMP DE MAI.

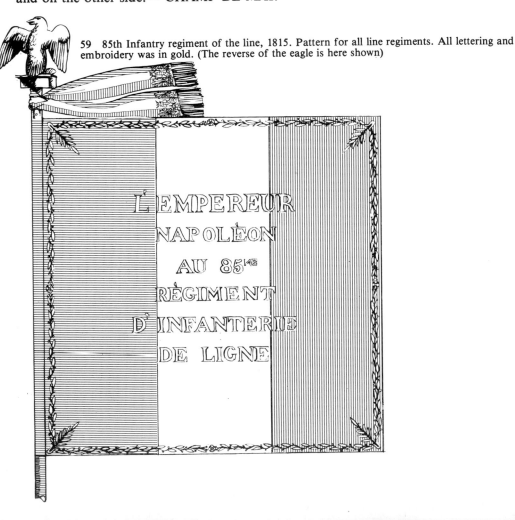

59   85th Infantry regiment of the line, 1815. Pattern for all line regiments. All lettering and embroidery was in gold. (The reverse of the eagle is here shown)

60 Marines of the Imperial Guard, 1804-1813. Colours the same as line flags. Eagle, anchor and crown all in gold. The other side did not have this badge but bore in the central lozenge the inscription:— L'EMPEREUR/DES FRANCAIS/AU Blon DE MARINS/DE LA GARDE/IMPERIALE. On the plinth of the eagle atop the staff was an anchor instead of the usual number.

61 1st Grenadiers of the Guard, 1811.

62 2nd Grenadiers of the Guard, 1813.

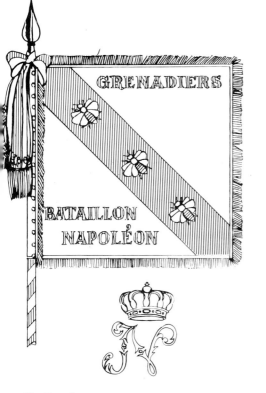

63 Battalion Napoleon, 1814. The other side did not have the lettering, and in place of bees the crowned 'N' (63a) in gold was borne in the centre of a crimson diagonal that ran from the upper staff corner to the lower fly.

As with the infantry arm there was no real standardisation of design for cavalry standards at the beginning of our period. Dragoons had guidons of the usual two-tailed shape, colours varying according to the squadron. The guidon for the 1st squadron of the 4th regiment was white with broad border of alternate blue and red squares. Lettering and grenades were gold. The guidon of the 4th squadron of the same regiment was red with a gold border, the inscriptions being the same as the 1st squadron. A drawing of a standard for hussars in 1803 shows a guidon with a simple semi-circular fly. The standard was divided horizontally, blue upper, red lower. The central device was a green, tightly-packed laurel wreath bound top and bottom with two turns of tricolour ribbon. The area within the wreath was white with a cock in natural colours, looking to the left, with wings partly displayed (like the imperial eagle) and standing on a golden trumpet. A tricolour ribbon lay across the bottom of the standard passing over the laurel, behind the trumpet and over the other arm of the laurel. This bore the inscription REPUBLIQUE to the left and FRANCAISE to the right of the laurel wreath. A scrollwork border in gold near the edge of the standard terminated in gold grenades in the staff side corners, and it had a gold fringe. A standard for the Cuirassiers of the same period was blue, and bore in the centre a cuirasse of Romanesque pattern in silver with red undercloth. Above this was a golden Romanesque helmet. The whole central motif was flanked by green laurel sprigs crossed at the bottom in the normal way. Above the helmet was a tricolour ribbon bearing the inscription REPUBLIQUE FRANCAISE. Below the laurel was another tricolour ribbon bearing the inscription:— (Number of Squadron) ER ESCADRON. A border of gold scrollwork had corners bearing the regimental number, the standard had a gold fringe on those three sides not attached to the staff.

The standards of 1804 were the same pattern as for the infantry. Two types were used by the cavalry; square (60cm. by 60cm.) and guidon (60cm. by 70cm.). Some individual examples are given below:—
The square standard of the first Cuirassiers bore in the corner wreaths the numeral I
The inscriptions were:—
L'EMPEREUR/DES FRANCAIS/AU ler REGIMENT/DE CUIRASSIERS
and on the other side:—
VALEUR/ET DISCIPLINE/2eme ESCADRON
The eagle bore the numeral I on the plinth. The 23rd regiment of Dragoons had a guidon (see illustration 65) in the usual colours.

The square standard of the 1st regiment of Hussars was the same design as that for the Cuirassiers with the inscription:—
L'EMPEREUR/DES FRANCAIS/AU ler REGIMENT/DE HUSSARDS
Inscription on the other side was exactly the same as the Cuirassier standard. All the regulations concerning the design and allocation of flags applied to the infantry were also applicable to the cavalry and other arms. In 1812 the tricolour standards of the cavalry were simply scaled-down versions of the infantry flag. Those of the first and second regiments had the following inscriptions:—

L'EMPEREUR/NAPOLEON/AU (number of regiment) REGIMENT/DE
CARABINIERS
on the other side the battle honours for both regiments were as follows:—
AUSTERLITZ/JENA/EYLAU/FRIEDLAND/ECKMUHL/WAGRAM
The following list gives the battle honours for the other regiments of line cavalry
starting with the Cuirassiers:—

1st regiment—ULM, AUSTERLITZ, JENA, EYLAU ECKMUHL, ESSLING, WAGRAM.
2nd regiment—AUSTERLITZ, FRIEDLAND, ECKMUHL, ESSLING, WAGRAM.
3rd regiment—AUSTERLITZ, JENA, EYLAU, FRIEDLAND, ECKMUHL, ESSLING, WAGRAM.
4th regiment—ESSLING, WAGRAM.
5th regiment—ULM, AUSTERLITZ, JENA, EYLAU, ECKMUHL, ESSLING, WAGRAM.
6th regiment—ESSLING, WAGRAM.
7th regiment—ESSLING, WAGRAM.
8th regiment—ESSLING, WAGRAM.
9th regiment—AUSTERLITZ, JENA, EYLAU, FRIEDLAND, ECKMUHL, WAGRAM.
10th regiment—ULM, AUSTERLITZ, JENA, EYLAU, ECKMUHL, ESSLING, WAGRAM.
11th regiment—ULM, AUSTERLITZ, JENA, EYLAU, ECKMUHL, ESSLING, WAGRAM.

The dragoon regiments:-
1st regiment—ULM, AUSTERLITZ, JENA, EYLAU, FRIEDLAND.
2nd regiment—ULM, AUSTERLITZ, JENA, EYLAU, FRIEDLAND.
3rd regiment—ULM, AUSTERLITZ, JENA, EYLAU, FRIEDLAND.
4th regiment—ULM, AUSTERLITZ, JENA, EYLAU, FRIEDLAND.
5th regiment—ULM, AUSTERLITZ, JENA, EYLAU.
6th regiment—ULM, AUSTERLITZ, JENA, EYLAU, FRIEDLAND.
8th regiment—ULM, AUSTERLITZ, JENA, EYLAU.
9th regiment—ULM, AUSTERLITZ, JENA, EYLAU.
10th regiment—ULM, AUSTERLITZ, JENA, EYLAU, FRIEDLAND.
11th regiment—ULM, AUSTERLITZ, JENA, EYLAU, FRIEDLAND.
12th regiment—ULM, AUSTERLITZ, JENA, EYLAU.
13th regiment—ULM, AUSTERLITZ, JENA, EYLAU.
(JENA was awarded in error as the regiment did not take part in this battle.)
14th regiment—ULM, AUSTERLITZ, JENA, EYLAU, FRIEDLAND.
15th regiment—ULM, AUSTERLITZ, JENA, EYLAU.
16th regiment—ULM, AUSTERLITZ, JENA, EYLAU.
17th regiment—ULM, AUSTERLITZ, JENA, EYLAU, FRIEDLAND.
18th regiment—ULM, AUSTERLITZ, JENA, EYLAU, FRIEDLAND.
19th regiment—ULM, AUSTERLITZ, JENA, EYLAU, FRIEDLAND.
20th regiment—ULM, AUSTERLITZ, JENA, EYLAU, FRIEDLAND.
21st regiment—ULM, JENA, EYLAU.
22nd regiment—ULM, AUSTERLITZ, JENA, EYLAU.
23rd regiment—WAGRAM.
24th regiment—WAGRAM.
25th regiment—ULM, AUSTERLITZ.
26th regiment—ULM, AUSTERLITZ, JENA, EYLAU, FRIEDLAND.
27th regiment—ULM, AUSTERLITZ, JENA, FRIEDLAND.
28th regiment—WAGRAM.
29th regiment—WAGRAM.
The 7th and 30th regiments were without battle honour inscriptions.

Chasseurs à cheval:-
1st regiment—AUSTERLITZ, JENA, EYLAU, ECKMUHL, WAGRAM.
2nd regiment—AUSTERLITZ, JENA, EYLAU, ECKMUHL, WAGRAM.
3rd regiment—FRIEDLAND, ECKMUHL, WAGRAM.
5th regiment—AUSTERLITZ, FRIEDLAND.
6th regiment—WAGRAM.
7th regiment—JENA, EYLAU, FRIEDLAND, ESSLING.
8th regiment—ULM, WAGRAM.
9th regiment—WAGRAM.
10th regiment—ULM, JENA, EYLAU, FRIEDLAND.
11th regiment—ULM, AUSTERLITZ, JENA, EYLAU, FRIEDLAND, ESSLING, WAGRAM.
12th regiment—AUSTERLITZ, JENA, EYLAU, ECKMUHL, WAGRAM.

13th regiment—ULM, AUSTERLITZ, EYLAU, FRIEDLAND, ESSLING, WAGRAM.
14th regiment—ECKMUHL, WAGRAM.
15th regiment—FRIEDLAND.
16th regiment—AUSTERLITZ, JENA, EYLAU, ECKMUHL, ESSLING, WAGRAM.
19th regiment—ECKMUHL, WAGRAM.
20th regiment—JENA, EYLAU, FRIEDLAND, ESSLING.
21st regiment—ULM.
22nd regiment—ULM, AUSTERLITZ, JENA, EYLAU, FRIEDLAND.
23rd regiment—ECKMUHL, ESSLING, WAGRAM.
24th regiment—FRIEDLAND, ESSLING, WAGRAM.
26th regiment—ULM, AUSTERLITZ.
Numbers 17 and 18 were vacant in the list, and regiments 4, 25 and 27 did not
have battle honour inscriptions.

Hussars:-
1st regiment—ULM, JENA, EYLAU, FRIEDLAND.
2nd regiment—AUSTERLITZ, JENA, FRIEDLAND.
3rd regiment—ULM, JENA, EYLAU, FRIEDLAND.
4th regiment—AUSTERLITZ, JENA, FRIEDLAND.
5th regiment—AUSTERLITZ, JENA, EYLAU, WAGRAM.
6th regiment—ULM, WAGRAM.
7th regiment—JENA, EYLAU, FRIEDLAND, WAGRAM.
8th regiment—ULM, AUSTERLITZ, JENA, EYLAU, ESSLING, WAGRAM.
9th regiment—ULM, AUSTERLITZ, FRIEDLAND, ESSLING.
10th regiment—ULM, AUSTERLITZ.

In 1811 an imperial decree called for the formation of nine regiments of Lancers.
The 1st, 2nd 3rd, 8th, 9th, 10th and 29th Dragoons, 1st and 2nd Polish Lancers,
and the 30th Chasseurs became respectively 1st, 2nd, 3rd, 4th, 5th, 6th, 7th, 8th,
and 9th Chevau-legers-Lanciers. The standards were of the regulation pattern and
the new regiments inherited the battle honours of the original regiment. Thus the
standard of the 3rd regiment of Chevau-legers-Lanciers bore the inscriptions:-
L'EMPEREUR/NAPOLEON/AU 3me REGIMENT/DE CHEVAU-LEGERS
and on the other side the battle honours:-
ULM/AUSTERLITZ/JENA, EYLAU
these being previously carried by the 8th regiment of Dragoons.

During the 1814 restoration standards of the cavalry were similar to those of
the infantry. The standard of the regiment 'de la Reine' (2nd Chasseurs) measured
55cm. by 55cm. The border of fleurs-de-lis and roses and the regimental number
in the corners, were in gold as on the infantry flags of the time. On one side was
the inscription:-
LE ROI/AU REGIMENT/DE LA REINE/2me/CHASSEURS
On the other side the central device consisted of the arms of France flanked by
laurel and oak branches in green, below which was a blue ribbon which probably
bore either a royalist inscription or a squadron number. The standard was edged
with a gold fringe.

The 1815 standards were again scaled down versions of the infantry flags but
the embroidered border was executed in the same size as on the infantry flags
and therefore looked proportionately larger on the smaller standards. Size was
55cm. square. Illustrated is the 1815 standard of the 6th regiment of the
Chasseurs à Cheval. The other side bore the single battle honour WAGRAM.

Other arms of the line had flags of corresponding type to the general pattern with their own inscriptions. The horse artillery carried guidons up to 1812.

Standards for the cavalry of the consular guard tended to be individual in their design like their infantry counterparts.

The 'Guides' (*Chasseurs à Cheval)* had a different standard for each squadron. The general design consisted of a square with a broad border. In the centre was the fascine, cap, and laurels as on the 1796 infantry flag. The word DISCIPLINE was parallel with the border on the staff side reading from the middle, and the word SUBORDINATION in the corresponding position on the fly side also reading from the centre. The word VIGILANCE was across the base between the centre device and the border. All lettering was gold with the centre device in the usual colours. The 1st squadron had a white field with a red border, the other squadrons had no borders, with blue field for the 2nd, green for the 3rd, and red for the 4th. All devices were the same as for the 1st squadron.

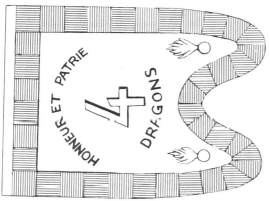

64   4th Dragoons of the line, pre-1804.

66   6th Chassuers à Cheval, 1815.

65   23rd Dragoons, 1804-1809. Other side was of the same design but inscription read:—
VALEUR/ET/DISCIPLINE/(No. of squadron)/ESCADRON.

The Artillery of the Guides had an oblong standard. This had a broad gold border with the centre portion divided horizontally, upper blue, lower white. Between the two inner corners of the borders on the fly was a red equilateral triangle, the third point of which rested on the line of division of the other two colours. Overall on the centre portion was the inscription in gold:-
PARTOUT/L'ATILLERIE/S'EST COMPLÉE/DE GLOIRE
The 1804 pattern for the Chasseurs à Cheval is illustrated. The other side bore within the central lozenge the inscription:-
L'EMPEREUR/DES FRANCAIS/AU REGIMENT DE CHASSEURS/À CHEVAL/DE LA GARDE/IMPERIALE
The standard for the 2nd regiment of Lancers was 60cm. square and had the number two in the corner wreaths. Inscriptions were as follows:-
GARDE/IMPERIALE/L'EMPEREUR/DES FRANCAIS/AU 2eme REGIMENT/DES CHEV. LÉGERS/LANCIERS
and on the other side:-
VALEUR/ET DISCIPLINE/ler ESCADRON
Also illustrated is the guidon for the Horse Artillery of the Guard. The other side bore the inscription:-
L'EMPEREUR/DES FRANCAIS/AU REGIMENT D'ARTILLERIE/Á CHEVAL/DE LA GARDE/IMPERIALE
In 1813 guard cavalry and artillery standards were exactly like those for the infantry of the guard but in the smaller size and with the relevant unit designation. It is assumed that standards for the hundred days were all similar to that already described for the Horse Artillery of the Guard in the guard infantry section.

68   Horse artillery of the Guard, 1806-13. Crowned eagle and crossed cannon badge all in gold. Other side bore the inscription as noted in text, only in the central lozenge. Plinth to eagle bore the words:— GARDE/IMPERIALE.

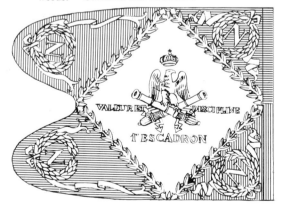

67   Chasseurs à Cheval of the Guard, 1804-13. Other side similar but with inscription, as noted in text, only within central lozenge. Coat of arms as shown was all in gold. Note wreath on eagle.

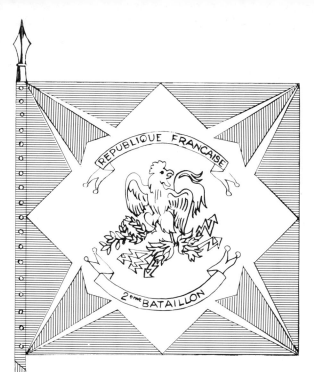

69   2nd regiment of the Vistula Legion (Polish troops in the French army), 1800-1813. Blue with white centre portion and red 'darts' pointing into corners. Cock in natural colours holding in one claw green laurels and in the other silver thunderbolts issuing from red and yellow flames. Light blue scrolls with gold lettering. Other side the same but with cock reversed so as to face fly on both sides. Staff red, white and blue hooped, and tipped with silver pike head.

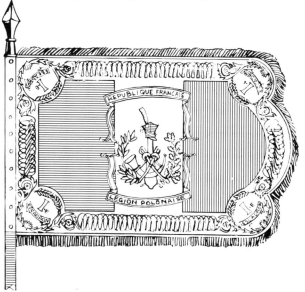

70   1st Regiment of Lancers of the Vistula Legion. Blue, white and red tricolour. White border and corners with gold embroidery and fringes. Central motif consisted of a brown club with a blue lancers' cap on top. The cap had a red plume and yellow cords. Crossed sabres and hunting horn were gold, tied with a green ribbon. Laurel branches were brown with green leaves. All scrolls were white with gold lettering. Corner designs had small green laurel branches spanning the open sides. On one side the lettering was in French as shown here but on the other in Polish. This read:— upper scroll, RJEEZYPOSPODITY FRANCONZKOY; lower scroll, LEGIO POLSKEIY. Corner scrolls SWADRON. All other details were the same on both sides except that, like the infantry flag, the central device was reversed to face the fly. Staff was blue, tipped with a silver spear point.

CI   Mecklemberg, 7th Rhinebund Regiment, 2nd battalion. 1st battalion the same but with white instead of blue background. 1808-1813.

C3   Spain. Infantry flag.

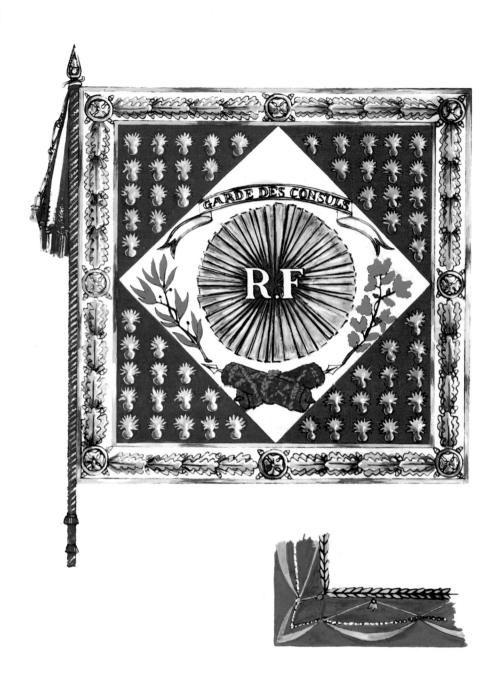

C2   France. Garde des Consuls. 1800-1804. C2a shows the border for the Chasseurs.

C4 Naples. 1807 model infantry flag. Other side has the same colouring but there are no wreaths or numbers in the corners. Instead of the arms the centre lozenge bore the inscription GIUSEPPE/NAPOLEONE/RE DELLE DUE SICILIE/AL Ime REGGIMENTO/D'INFANTERIA/LEGGERA (or DE LINEA for line infantry regiments).

C6 Brunswick coat of arms.

C5   Hesse. Standard Leibgarde zu Pferde.   This measured 56 by 54cm.

C10   a and b, Arms and monogram as on Saxon flags.

C7 Hesse-Darmstadt Leib-regiment ordinary flag

C11 Arms of Bavaria.

C8   Austria 1806 Infantry flag.

C9   Wurtzburg. Reverse of infantry flag. A drawing of the other side appears in the text.

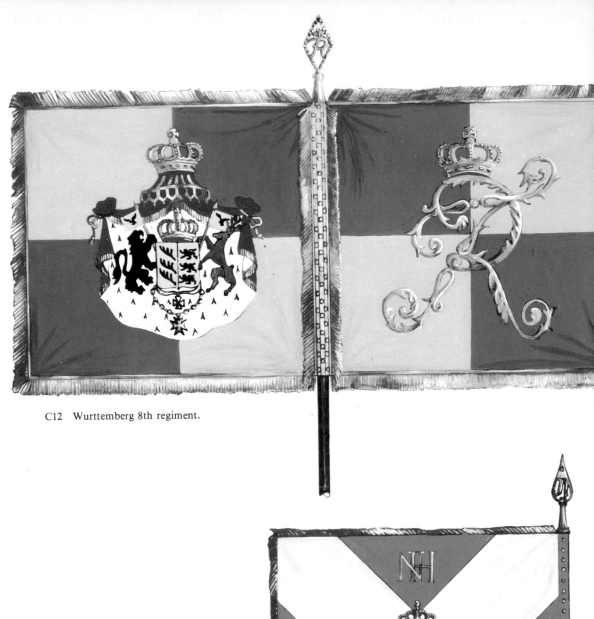

C12　Wurttemberg 8th regiment.

C13　Westphalia 1812 Guard infantry flag.

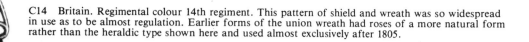

C14 Britain. Regimental colour 14th regiment. This pattern of shield and wreath was so widespread in use as to be almost regulation. Earlier forms of the union wreath had roses of a more natural form rather than the heraldic type shown here and used almost exclusively after 1805.

C15 Russia, Cavalry standard.

Hanover

The new Hanoverian army of 1813 had flags of individual regimental design. What details that are known are listed below.

Feldbataillon Hoya (formally Langenehr and earlier still Roehl): Both sides were black and on one side there was a white upright sword superimposed over a white oak wreath. The other side was an iron cross with the inscription 'MIT GOTT FURS VATERLAND'. The blue staff had a spear point with an iron cross thereon. Feldbataillon Calenberg: 126cm. by 128cm. white fringed cloth. On both sides were wreaths of oak and laurel leaves with on one side the inscription within 'ZIEHT AUS ZUM EDLEN-KAMPF' and on the other 'KEHRT-HEIMMIT-SIEG-GEKROENET'. Below the confluence of the wreath arms was the notation 'AO 1813'. The pike head bore the royal initials within an oval chain loop and the flag had cords and tassels.

Of an unknown unit a white flag of similar size to that of the Calenberg regiment and also with a fringe. On one side the white horse of Hanover on a red circle, surrounded by a border bearing the inscription 'QUO FAST ET GLORIA DUCUNT'. On the other side a white central circle surrounded by a red embroidered border. Within the circle a crowned GR III cypher.

Landwehr Bataillon Gifhorn. Only certain details are known of this flag. It was yellow, measured 100cm. by 180cm. and was fringed. The central design was an oak tree in front of which was a crowned, leaping horse of Hanover (facing the fly) in silver. Below this was an inscription of which the last word was 'Gifhorn' but the rest is unknown. Staff was blue, and yellow cords and tassels were attached. It is possible that this flag, together with another known item for the Landwehr bataillon Osnabruck, was presented after 1815 and thus out of our period.

71   Hanover Feldbataillon Calenberg, 1813.

72 Hanover Infantry regiment flag, 1813.

Hesse-Darmstadt

The Grand Dutchy of Hesse contributed three infantry regiments to the Confederation of the Rhine. These were the Leib-Garde, Leib regiment and the Erbprinz (Hertier) regiment. Two flags were carried for each battalion by senior NCOs. The flags measured 130cm. by 130cm. on a staff 315cm. long. As each was two battalions strong the regiments had four flags for Leib and Leib-Guard and for Erbprinz. All were of similar design but the first flag of the 1st battalion in the Leib and Erbprinz regiments had a white field with corners only in the regimental colours. The other three colours in each case had the regimental colours taking up the whole field. Thus the colours of the flags for the three regiments were as follows:—

Leib-Garde
: Four flags all exactly the same. White field, no corner rays. Red and white lion crowned gold on light blue background bordered by green laurel wreath bearing red fruit. Ribbon red with PRO PATRIA in gold. Gold crown with red lining and white pearls. Ribbon tying laurel white, edged in red. Corner devices, gold monogram enclosed by green laurel bearing red fruit and tied by pink ribbon. Crown gold with red lining and white pearls. Grenades silver. White staff.

Leib-regiment
: 1st (Company) flag: White field with half black, half red corner rays. The area enclosed within the wreaths in the corners was white. Grenades red and silver mixed.

Erbprinz regiment

The other three flags. Black field with corner rays red. All other colourings as per the 1st flag. Staffs brown.

1st (Company) flag. White field with pink and black corner rays. All other colourings as per Leib-regiment. The other flag (only one other carried) black with pink corner rays, otherwise the same. White staffs. In 1804, with the addition of a 2nd battalion, the colours of this regiment changed and the four new flags were as follows:—

1st (Company) flag, white with half black, half yellow corner rays. All other colours remained unchanged except that the backgrounds to the corner monograms were no longer white but allowed the yellow and black to show through, and the upper ribbon was white and the lower pink on the central device. The other three colours were black with yellow corner rays and all other details were as the 1st flag. Staffs were black.

All flags had white tassels on the end of white cravats decorated with two lines of colours. These were:— Leib-regiment and Leib-Garde red and blue mixed, Erbprinz red and yellow mixed (on the earlier flag pink and black). The Erbprinz regiment lost two of its flags (2nd/1st bttn., 1st/2nd bttn.) to the British at Badajoz in 1812; the Leib-regiment lost one (2nd/2nd bttn.) to the Austrians at Wagram in 1809.

73   Hesse-Darmstadt Company flag Leib-Regimant, 1806-14. Pattern similar for all regiments.

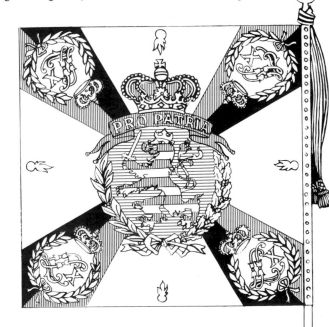

After the retreat from Russia the regiments were rebuilt and during the 1813 campaign they carried the following flags:—
1st battalion the Leib-Garde-Leibfahne
2nd battalion the Leib-Garde-Retierfahne
1st battalion the Leib-Regiment-Leibfahne
2nd battalion the Leib-Regiment-Retierfahne (of the first battalion).

In 1814 new flags were presented to the reconstituted army. These measured 112cm. by 109cm. and the design was similar to those carried previously except that the central wreath was now made up of one arm of laurels (the left) and one of oak leaves. The ribbon across to the top of the central device was now black edged in red, and bore the inscription 'Fur Gott, Ehre Vaterland'. The wreaths to the corner cyphers were of laurel and oak like the central wreath. The regimental colours were as follows:—

1st and 2nd bttns. Leib-Garde-Rgt. . . . . White
1st and 2nd bttns. Garde-Fus-Rgt. . . . . White with red corners
1st bttn. Leib-Rgt. . . . . White; half pink, half black corners
2nd bttn. Leib-Rgt. . . . . Black with pink corners
1st bttn. Gross und Erbprinz Rgt. . . . . White; half yellow, half black corners
2nd bttn. Gross und Erbprinz Rgt. . . . . Black with yellow corners
1st bttn. Prinz Emil Rgt. . . . . White; half blue, half black corners
2nd bttn. Prinz Emil Rgt. . . . . Black with blue corners.

The Chevau-Legers had no standards but the Leih-Garde zu Pferde carried one that had been presented to them in 1770 (see colour section).

Hesse-Kassel

Four battalions of Landwehr were raised for the fight against Napoleon. These carried flags, one of which is described here:

Red cloth, in the centre a blue escutcheon with a gold Landwehr cross thereon. The cross bore inscriptions. Above this shield was a crown in gold between the two arms of a wreath, also in gold, which surrounded the shield. In the corners were radiating lines, alternately long and short, the longer lines having arrow heads, all in gold. The staff was surmounted by a gilt tip.

74 Hesse-Kassel Landwehr, 1813.

Holland

When Louis Napoleon became King of Holland in 1806 he required a new design for the flags of the army. After several trial patterns the design here illustrated was settled upon in December 1806. The particular flag illustrated was captured by the British at Veere in 1809. It measured 80cm. by 80cm. and the border was divided up into segments of red and blue. The central area was white. The lion was in natural colours on a green field, held a silver sword and arrows, and was crowned with a gold crown which had a red lining and blue 'pearls' on the arches. All lettering on both sides was gold.

Details of another Dutch flag taken in 1809 describe a white flag with gold cords and tassels. In the centre was a gold lion laying amidst a trophy of arms. The lion was laying to the right but its head was turned so that it was looking to the left over its back. The trophy of arms consisted of flags arrayed to the left and right, one red, two white, one blue, one red and white, plus a pink vexillum type (six in all). The lower part of the trophy consisted of various swords, spears, bayonets, drums and cannon barrels, all pointing outwards from a centre point behind the lion. Behind the lion in a central vertical position was a silver fascine, bound gold and topped by a liberty cap. This cap was coloured, top half red, lower half silver. A similar flag but with a blue background is also known but unfortunately there is no information as to the unit. It has been suggested that these flags belonged to Swiss units in the Dutch service.

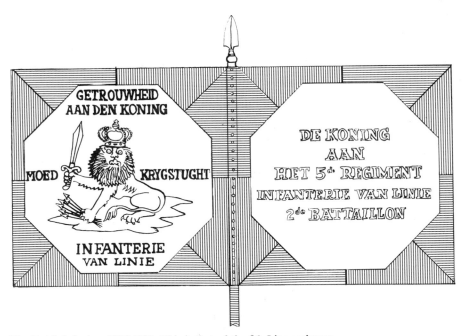

75   Dutch infantry, 1806-1810. This is that of the 5th Line regiment.

Italy

There is some confusion concerning the pattern of flags and standards for the line regiments of the Kingdom of Italy. In 1805 when Italy became a Kingdom, a pattern was submitted to Napoleon which was similar to the French 1804 model but which had on one side a globe and on the reverse an eagle surrounded by a mantle. The flag staff was surmounted by an Italian-style eagle looking to the right. According to many references this pattern of flag was never adopted but flags of the French pattern (as issued to the Italian Guard regiments who were in France at the time) were decreed for all units. There is evidence that both types existed, but whether one type was replaced by the other or one type was manufactured but not issued is not clear. I would think it is quite possible that the Italian type was used from about 1808 (design disagreements apparently causing delays) and was possibly replaced by the French type in 1812/13.

The flag issued to the infantry of the Royal Guard in 1805 was as shown in the illustration (76). It measured 86cm. by 80cm. The upper corner triangle nearest the staff and the lower fly corner were green with the lower staff and upper fly red. Central lozenge was white. All laurels, grenades and inscriptions were in gold. The opposite side was similar but the inscription was as follows:-
GARDE ROIALE/VALEUR/ET DISCIPLINE
This flag was replaced by another which was similar but has the inscriptions in Italian as follows:-
NAPOLEONE IMPERATORE/E RE/AL PIEDI DELLA GUARDIA/REALE
and on the obverse:-
GUARDIA REALE/VALORE/E DISCIPLINA
The Guard Cacciatori had a flag of the same design but with bugle horns in place of the grenades and laurels in the corners, and the word 'Cacciatori' replaced the word 'Granatieri' in the inscription.

A new model was issued in 1814. This measured 80cm. by 80cm. The basic colour scheme was the same as the preceding flag with the additions of eagle, star and crown in gold, the latter with red and green gems. Laurel and oak sprays were in natural colours. The ribbon was blue with gold lettering.

The line infantry in 1804 was issued with a flag that had all four corners red, centre lozenge white with a green square filling the centre thus forming four white triangles. These flags were replaced in 1805 because the earlier pattern bore republican inscriptions. If it is to be assumed that the Italian pattern was used, then it is possible that from 1805 to 1808 (when the Italian design was finalised) the line infantry carried no flags. The colours were the same as Guard flags but with a blue globe in the centre of the lozenge on one side. This was surrounded by golden rays and was encompassed by the laurel and oak branches as on the Guard 1813 standard. The globe carried an inscription in gold as follows:-
NAPOLEONE/IMPERATORE DE FRANCESI/RE D'ITALIA/AL (number of regiment) REGGto. D'INFANTERIA/DELLA LINEA

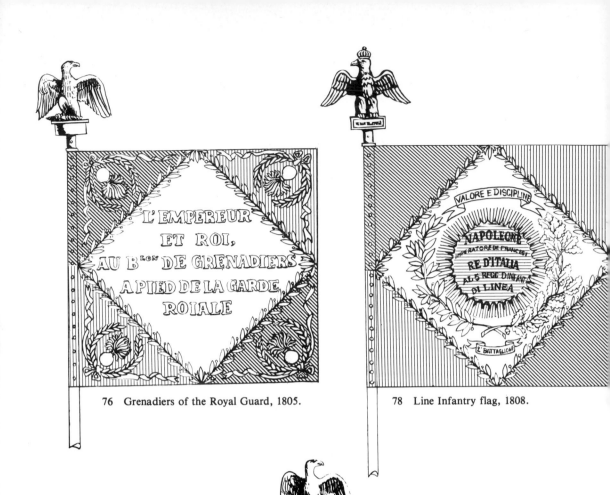

76 Grenadiers of the Royal Guard, 1805.

78 Line Infantry flag, 1808.

77 Grenadiers of the Royal Guard, 1813.

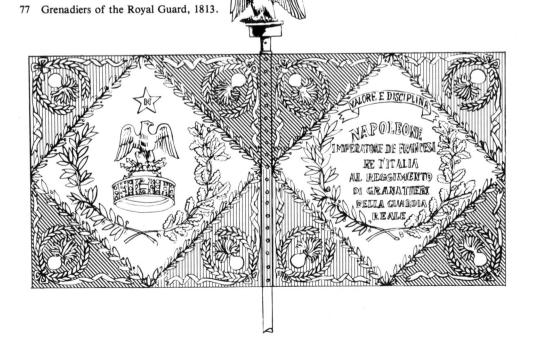

Blue scrolls above and below the globe bore the wording in gold:-
VALORE E DISCIPLINE and on the lower (number of battalion)
BATTAGLIONE.
The obverse had the royal arms as per the Dragoons standard but with green
mantle and red field to breast shield. The corner triangles were plain on the globe
side but contained laurel wreaths of the usual pattern on the royal arms side.

The French pattern was similar to the Italian design in basic configuration but
the devices were different. On one side (as illustrated in fig.79) a golden eagle
with red oval bearing a gold crown was displayed below a gold crown. Ribbons
were blue with gold lettering. Other side was similar but simply bore the
inscription:-
NAPOLEONE/IMPERATORE E RE/AL (number of regiment)
REGGIMENTO/FANTERIA/DI LINEA (or LEGGERA for light infantry)
Early flags were embroidered but after 1813 (the time the French patterns were
issued?) all were painted.

79   Line Infantry flag, 1813.

The cavalry standards followed roughly the same patterns as the infantry flags.
The Royal Guard Cavalry consisted of three regiments, Dragoni della Guardia,
Gendarmeria Scelta della Guardia Real and Guardi d'Onore.
The 1805 to 1813 standard for the Dragoni della Guardia measured 60cm. by
60cm. and is shown in the illustration. The coat of arms normally consisted of an
ermine-lined green mantle with gold eagle, fringe to mantle crown and all other

details. The halberd heads were silver and the shield was red with a gold crown. The small shield was white with a gold 'N' as was the star. The mantle however is often depicted gold and sometimes the background to the shield is shown white.

The other side bore the blue globe as per the Italian-style infantry flag. The inscription on the globe read as follows:—

NAPOLEONE/IMPERATORE DE FRANCESI/RE D'ITALIA/AL DRAGONI/DELLA GUARDIA/REALE

The globe was flanked by the laurel and oak leaves, and had blue scrolls top and bottom. The upper read VALORE E DISCIPLINA, the lower (No. of squadron) SQUADRONE.

In 1813 this standard was replaced by a new model which measured 56cm. by 56cm. This was similar to that shown for the Cacciatori regiments but the inscription read:—

NAPOLEONE/IMPERATORE E RE/AL DRAGONI/DELLA GUARDIA/REALE

The only other difference from the Cacciatori standard was that the bugle horn decoration in the corners was replaced by an 'N' within a laurel as on the earlier standard.

The Gendarmeria Scelta carried a standard as illustrated. This measured 60cm. by 60cm. The colours were the same as for the infantry flags with the exceptions of the grenades and fringes which were silver on this standard.

The Guardi Reali d'Onore standard (1813) measured 56cm. by 56cm. The colours are the same as the preceding standards with gold corner decorations and fringes. The standards of the line cavalry followed basically the same pattern as those of the Guard.

The standards of the regiments of Cacciatori a Cavallo were as shown and measured 56cm. by 56cm. Colours were the same as the preceding standards. A variation in the inscription ran as follows:—

NAPOLEONE/IMPERATORE E RE/AL 20 REGGo CACCIATORI/A CAVILLO/PRINCIPE REALE

The regiments of Dragoons had two types of standards; one large per regiment and one small per squadron. Both types had the same design and this was like the infantry pattern with the globe. The globe bore the following inscription:—

NAPOLEONE/IMPERATORE DE FRANCESI/RE D'ITALIA/AL REGGIMENTO/DRAGONI/NAPOLEONE

The ribbons bore, on the upper VALORE E DISCIPLINA and on the lower NEL TUO NOME VITTORIOSI. The corners were decorated with 'N's within laurels. A squadron standard of the Regina regiment had the following inscription on the globe:—

NAPOLEONE/IMPERATORE DE FRANCESI/RE D'ITALIA/AL REGGTo DE DRAGONI/DELLA REGINA

The lower ribbon bore the lettering 40 SQUADRONE. In 1813 these standards were replaced by a new pattern like that shown for the Gendarmeria Scelta but without a fringe and the grenades replaced by gold 'N's within the laurels. The inscription was as follows:—

NAPOLEONE/IMPERATORE DE FRANCESI/RE d'ITALIA/AL REGGTo DRAGONI/DELLA REGINA

The upper scroll bore VALORE E DISCIPLINA, the lower (number of squadron) SQUAD.NE.

The Dragoni Napoleone regiment standard of 1813 measured 56cm. square. On one side was the coat of arms and the crowned 'N's the same as that of the Guardi Reali d'Onore. The other side bore the laurel and oak sprays as per the Gendarmeria Scelta but with the inscription:—

DRAGONI/NAPOLEONE/(number of squadron) SQUADne

The other cavalry standard illustrated is that of the 2nd regiment of Hussars of the Cisalpine Republic, 1800 to 1801. The basic colour of the standard was white. The border was made up of alternate green and red triangles facing inwards, thus forming white triangles facing outwards. The first triangle in the upper row near the pole was green, the rest following in sequence. The rectangle nearest the pole was green, that near the fly red, thus leaving a white centre panel. The brown sticks were bound by a tricolour ribbon. The revolutionary bonnet was red. Laurel and oak leaves were green (of a different shade to the green particoloured section). The two scrolls were white with red lettering.

80   Dragoons of the Guard, 1805-1813.

The foot artillery flag was of infantry pattern with the blue globe bearing the inscription:—
NAPOLEONE/IMPERATORE DE FRANCESI/RE D'ITALIA/AL 10 REGGIMENTO/D'ARTIGLIERA
The scrolls were silver and gold. This flag was probably replaced in 1813 by one of the later pattern. The horse artillery had a standard of the same pattern with the inscription the same as above but the number 1° was replaced by 2°. This

81   Gendameria Scelta, 1810.

82   Guard of Honour, 1813.

standard was replaced in 1813 by one of the same pattern as that described for the Cavallo Cacciatori. The inscription was as follows:—
NAPOLEONE/IMPERATORE E RE/AL REGGIMENTO/D'ARTIGLIERA/A CAVALLO
The scrolls above the eagle bore the word VALORE, that below the eagle E DISCIPLINA. Instead of the bugle horns in the corners there were gold crossed cannon barrels with the crown above, at the same angle as the former devices.

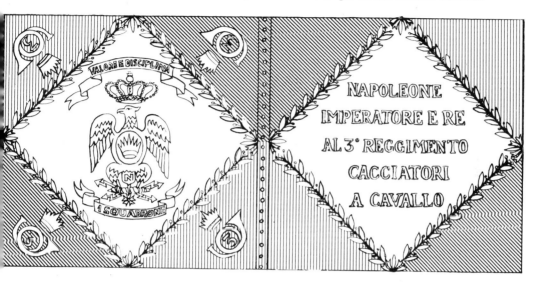

83   Light cavalry, 1813.

84   2nd regiment of hussars of the Cisalpine Republic, 1800 to 1801.

Mecklembourg

In 1808 Mecklembourg supplied troops to form the 7th regiment of the Confederation of the Rhine. The unit was formed of personnel from the three regiments of Mecklembourg-Schwerin. These three regiments had each carried two flags, a white 'Avancierfahne' and a blue 'Retirierfahne'. The two battalions of the 7th Rhinebunde regiment received one flag each. The 1st battalion had the white 1797 pattern flag of the old regiment von Hobe, and the 2nd battalion received the blue 1797 flag of the old regiment Erbprinz. The flags were exactly the same in design with only the colour of the background being different. They measured 90cm. high by 110cm. long and the pike head was gilt. This unit was destroyed in 1812.

In 1810 a Grenadier-Guard-Battalion was raised for the home establishment, eventually joining forces with the allies in 1813 against Napoleon. In 1810 it was presented with a flag of white cloth bearing a similar design to that of the Rhinebund regiment, but with the arms on a square rather than an oval shield. Corner cyphers were surrounded by wreaths consisting of palm leaves for one arm, laurel leaves for the other.

A regiment of Jager zu Pferde in 1813, was presented with an embroidered standard of white cloth with, on one side the inscription:— 'Von Gott kommt Muth und Starke' in gold within a gold oak wreath; and on the other, the arms of Mecklembourg in natural colours within a gold oak wreath, all superimposed on a red cross.

Naples

Under Joseph Napoleon the army of Naples had a flag similar to the French 1804 pattern. This flag was issued in 1807 and measured 80cm. by 80cm. It was carried by an officer of the lower ranks and was attached to a black painted staff which was surmounted by a brass pike head. One flag was permitted to each battalion. The flag itself had black and red triangles in place of the French red and blue, the red being situated in the upper staff and lower fly corners on both sides, the black occupying the other two corners. In the centre of the white lozenge on one side was the coat of arms of Naples. The coat of arms was surrounded by an ermine-lined, light blue mantle which had a chequered white and light crimson border and a gold fringe. Above this was a gold crown. The mermaids to left and right were in natural colours. The chain of the order (Légion d'Honneur) was gold, the cross white. All other decoration was gold. The other side was similar but without the corner wreaths and regimental numbers. The central lozenge bore in place of the coat of arms the inscription:—
GIUSSEPE/NAPOLEONE/RE DELLE DUE SICILIE/AL (number of regiment)
REGGIMENTO/D'INFANTERIA/DI LINEA (or LEGGERA for light infantry)

85 Infantry flag, 1809.

Fringe was gold.

When Murat became King he greatly enlarged the army and also redesigned the flags. In 1809 the new model was introduced, being issued to the third and fourth infantry regiments. The first and second regiments, then in Spain, did not receive their new flags until 1810. The new regiments were issued with flags as they were raised. As before they were carried by a junior officer but now measured 85cm. by 78cm. (with the exception of the flag of the 5th regiment of line which for some reason had a flag of the regulation design but measuring 118cm. by 114cm.). The earlier pike head was now replaced by a prancing horse. For all regiments (with the exception of the 6th of the line) the colour of the field was light blue. There was a border of light crimson and white checks near the edge. Within this border on one side was a wreath made up of oak leaves (right arm) and laurel leaves (left arm) tied with a gold ribbon and within this laurel was the regimental designation in gold. These designations varied slightly and where known are listed below:—

4th line:—

AL REGGto/D'INFANTERIA/40 DI LINEA

5th line:—
AL REGGto/REAL/CALABRIA/50 DI LINEA
6th line:—
AL/REGGIMENTO/DI NAPOLI/60 DI LINEA
7th line:—
AL 70/REGGIMENTO/FANTERIU/DI LINEA
In each case the entwined NG and the crown, all in gold, surmounted the inscription. On the other side within the border was a coat of arms with two mermaids in proper colours as supporters. The arms themselves had a broad gold border and were divided thus:— In chief a blue field with golden imperial eagle lower left, yellow with a black prancing horse, lower right, yellow with three legs and a face at their junction all in proper colours. Around this was the chain and order of the two Sicilies in gold. Over all was the golden crown. Cravat was light blue with light crimson and white checked band and golden fringe. Cords and tassels were gold. Staffs were mid blue.

It seems that the sixth regiment had a flag that conformed to the regulation in every way except that the background colour of flag and cravat was crimson instead of light blue. It seems that the staff of this flag was painted in spirals of a three colour combination possibly of light crimson, white and deep crimson or light blue.

Nassau

It seems that only one design of flag was carried during the Napoleonic wars. This dated from about 1810 and was carried throughout the conflict, first in the service of Napoleon and then against him at Waterloo where a flag of this pattern is known to have been carried by at least the 2nd light Infantry regiment of Nassau.

86 Nassau Infantry flag. This was yellow with a blue central disc scattered with golden billets (rectangles). A crowned golden lion rampant was in the centre of this field. The whole design was surrounded by a green laurel wreath. Staff was tipped with a gold spear point and gold cords and tassels were attached.

Portugal

There is not much information available on the flags carried during the Napoleonic Wars and some details conflict. In 1806 each regiment carried two types of flag—a King's flag with the colours red and blue forming a sixteen-part field, and a battalion flag which was in the colour of the division to which the regiment belonged. The army of that time was divided into three divisions, North, Centre and South, which had the distinctive colours of yellow, white and red respectively. These distinctive colours were shown on the lining of the troops' coats with regimental distinctions being by the colour of the collars and cuffs. The regimental flags had attached cravats of the colour of the regimental facings. The following descriptive notes are on several flags of the time:—

King's flag 24th Infantry regiment. This is similar to the flag illustrated for the 9th regiment. Field divided into sixteen parts red and blue with overall a yellow diagonal cross. The royal arms were in the centre on a white ground. Small white squares in the corners bore the monogram of the Prince Regent. Scroll below the central device was blue.

Regimental flags of the 6th, 8th, 9th and 10th Infantry regiments. These are coloured red, yellow and white respectively. All designs as described for the King's colour above were carried directly on the background colour. Another reference gives the colour of the 6th regiment flag as yellow.

King's flag of the Militia regiment Figueira. Field of sixteen blue, red and yellow with white diagonal cross. In the centre the Royal arms on a white field. Below the Central device was a blue scroll with the inscription REGIMENTO DE MILICIAS DE FIGUEIRA in yellow. In the corners the usual cyphers. After 1808 militia, King's and regimental flags were of the same design as those of the line.

King's flag of the Company of Ordenancas of Pedourido. Field of sixteen in red and blue with a blue border. A white diagonal cross. Central device royal arms on white ground. Below this a blue scroll with the inscription C.DE ORDENANCAS DE PEDOURIDO in yellow. Corner cyphers as before.

Flags issued in 1814 followed similar lines but the scroll below the cypher was now white with black lettering. The flags illustrated for the Cacadores and the 21st Infantry regiments differ from the others shown and possibly were of a later issue. Note the two different patterns shown for the same regiment (the 7th Cacadores).

Cavalry standards were white, red, yellow and blue for the 1st, 2nd, 3rd, and 4th squadron of each regiment respectively. The royal arm with trophies as on the infantry flags formed the central device but without the encircling motto band. Beneath the centre was a blue scroll with the unit designation in yellow letters thereon. As for the infantry the cravats were in the regimental facing colour.

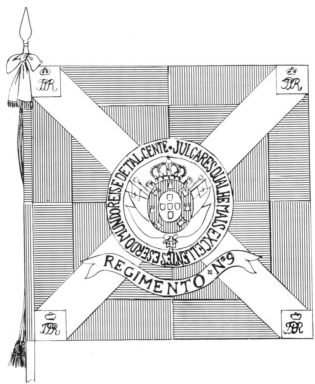

87 King's flag, 9th Infantry regiment. Horizontal shading indicates blue areas, vertical red. Cross was yellow. Centre white with white surrounding band carrying black lettering. Scroll white with black lettering. Corner squares white with gold monogrammes. Central arms in proper colour. Gold crown and cannons, black rammers. Flags top to bottom on both sides were:— white with red cross, plain red, plain blue. Red oval with gold castles. White centre with five blue shields. Gold tip with gold cravat and cords.

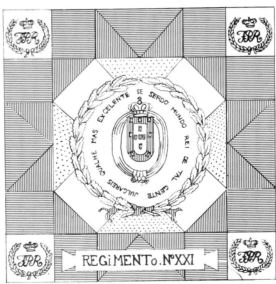

90 King's flag, 21st Infantry regiment. Colours as fig. 89 with the addition of yellow sections in the design, here indicated by the dotted areas.

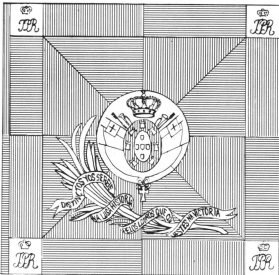

88 and 89   King's flag 7th and 11th Cazadores. Colours as before with the addition of a green oak wreath and four medals the ribbons for which passed around the central device. These ribbons were, from the outside toward the centre, green, orange, red and blue.

Prussia

The design and issue of flags and standards for the Prussian army of the Napoleonic wars fall into two distinct periods: pre 1806 and post 1806. Before the collapse of the Prussian army in 1806 the flags and standards were virtually the same as in Frederick the Great's time. The regiments each had two flags per battalion. The first flag of the first battalion was the Leibfahne, the second a Regimentsfahne. The second battalion had two Regimentsfahnen. Altogether the infantry had 236 flags, the three musketeer battalions and two interim companies of the 60th regiment did not have flags at this time. The flags were carried by senior NCOs and in most cases the staff head was gilt (the Guard regiments had silver when they were raised but were later replaced with gilt). Staff heads were spear shaped and pierced with the royal monogram as per the corner medallions of the flags. Ribbons and tassels were silver with black stripes in all cases. The Leibfahne was usually in reversed colours.

The following list is of infantry flags in 1806:—
Unless otherwise noted the eagles are black and in most cases the scroll is in the ground colour. In the cases where flags bear a cross, either straight or wavy, the cross is upright. Thus for straight crosses the ground colour only shows in the form of corner rays. The wavy cross covers a much smaller area and thus the bulk of the flag shows the ground colour.

Flagstaffs were light brown with the following exceptions:—
6th regiment, yellow; 15th regiment, white; 45th regiment, black.

Regiment number	Flag	Ground colour	Centre	Embroidery	Cross
1	LF	white	orange	silver	none
,,	RF	orange	white	silver	none
2	LF	white	black	gold (inc. eagle)	none
,,	RF	black	white	gold	none
3	LF	white	yellow	silver	none
,,	RF	yellow	white	silver	none
4	LF	white	crimson	gold	yellow wavy
,,	RF	crimson	white	gold	yellow wavy
5	LF	white	yellow	gold	red wavy
,,	RF	yellow	white	gold	red wavy
6	LF	white	white	gold	none
,,	RF	white	blue	gold	none
7	LF	crimson	blue	silver	white straight
,,	RF	crimson	white	silver	blue straight
8	LF	white	black	gold (inc. eagle)	black wavy
,,	RF	black	white	gold	white wavy
9	LF	white	green	gold	crimson wavy
,,	RF	green	white	gold	crimson wavy
10	LF	white	light green	gold	none
,,	RF	light green	white	gold	none
11	LF	white	crimson	gold	crimson wavy
,,	RF	crimson	white	gold	white wavy
12	LF	light green	light green	gold	white straight
,,	RF	white	white	gold	light green straight

100 Leibfahne, pre-1806. Here shown with large cross with wavy sides as per regiment No. 46. The central and corner devices were the same for all regiments with one or two exceptions as indicated in the list for 1806.

Regiment number	Flag	Ground colour	Centre	Embroidery	Cross
13	LF	crimson	black	silver (inc. eagle)	white straight
,,	RF	crimson	white	silver	black straight
14	LF	white	crimson	gold	none
,,	RF	crimson	white	gold	none
15	LF	white with vertical silver stripes	silver	silver	(this flag was of an individual design)
,,	RF	(as Leibfahn but with blue centre)			
16	LF	white	orange	gold	orange wavy
,,	RF	orange	white	gold	white navy
17	LF	crimson	crimson	gold	white straight
,,	RF	white	white	gold	crimson straight
18	LF	red	blue	silver	white large cross with curved sides
,,	RF	red	white	silver	blue large cross with curved sides
19	LF	white	crimson	gold	crimson maltese cross
,,	RF	crimson	white	gold	white maltese cross
20	LF	white	turquoise	gold	none
,,	RF	turquoise	white	gold	none
21	LF	white	crimson	gold	black wavy
,,	RF	crimson	white	gold	black wavy
(also two side 'flames' carrying to the left the initials CWF. to the right HZB)					
22	LF	white	blue	gold	red wavy
,,	RF	blue	white	gold	red wavy
23	LF	white	white	silver	none
,,	RF	white	blue	silver	none
(the corner medallions to both designs had a blue background in this regiment)					
24	LF	white	green	gold	green wavy
,,	RF	green	white	gold	white wavy
25	LF	yellow	green	gold	white straight
,,	RF	yellow	white	gold	green straight
26	LF	white	yellow	silver	yellow wavy
,,	RF	yellow	white	silver	white wavy
27	LF	white	blue	gold	yellow wavy down crimson wavy across
,,	RF	blue	white	gold	,, ,, ,,
28	LF	blue	black	gold (inc. eagle)	white straight
,,	RF	blue	white	gold	black straight
29	LF	yellow	blue	gold	white straight
,,	RF	yellow	white	gold	blue straight
30	LF	black	green	gold	white straight
,,	RF	black	white	gold	green straight
31	LF	blue	blue	gold	white straight
,,	RF	white	white	gold	blue straight
32	LF	red	blue	gold	white straight and black wavy
,,	RF	red	white	gold	blue straight and black wavy
33	LF	white	blue	silver	none
,,	RF	blue	white	silver	none
34	LF	white	blue	silver	narrow blue cross
,,	RF	blue	white	silver	white straight and narrow blue cross
35	LF	white	light blue	silver	none
,,	RF	light blue	white	silver	none
36	LF	white	lilac	gold	none
,,	RF	lilac	white	gold	none

Regiment number	Flag	Ground colour	Centre	Embroidery	Cross
37	LF	white	lime green	gold	none
,,	RF	lime green	white	gold	none
38	LF	white	red	gold	none
,,	RF	red	white	gold	none
39	LF	yellow	yellow	silver	white straight
,,	RF	white	white	silver	yellow straight
40	LF	white	deep pink	gold	Design of centre
,,	RF	deep pink	white	gold	wreath individual to this regiment; it was surrounded by a circle consisting of alternate medallions and black eagles
41	LF	white	yellow	silver	none
,,	RF	yellow	white	silver	none
42	LF	orange	orange	gold	white straight
,,	RF	white	white	gold	orange straight
43	LF	white	light green	gold	none
,,	RF	light green	white	gold	none
44	LF	red	light blue	gold	white straight
,,	RF	red	white	gold	light blue straight
45	LF	orange	blue	gold	white straight
,,	RF	orange	white	gold	blue straight
46	LF	black	yellow	gold	white, large cross with curved sides
,,	RF	black	white	gold	yellow, large cross with curved sides
48	LF	light blue	crimson	silver	white straight
,,	RF	light blue	white	silver	crimson straight
49	LF	white	beige	silver	none
,,	RF	beige	white	silver	none
50	LF	crimson	blue	gold	white straight
,,	RF	crimson	white	gold	blue straight
51	LF	light blue	yellow	silver	white straight
,,	RF	light blue	white	silver	yellow straight
52	LF	white	dark green	silver	poppy red wavy
,,	RF	dark green	white	silver	poppy red wavy
53	LF	red	light green	silver	white straight
,,	RF	red	white	silver	light green straight
54	LF	white	black	gold (inc. eagle)	red wavy
,,	RF	black	white	gold	red wavy
55	LF	white	light blue	silver	yellow wavy
,,	RF	light blue	white	silver	yellow wavy
56	LF	crimson	green	silver	white, large cross with curved sides
,,	RF	crimson	white	silver	green, large cross with curved sides
57	LF	white	—	gold	none
,,	RF	deep pink	—	gold	none
58	LF	yellow	yellow	silver	white straight
,,	RF	yellow	yellow	silver	light blue straight
59	LF	light blue	light blue	gold	white straight
,,	RF	white	white	gold	light blue straight
60	No flags issued at this time.				

Large numbers of flags were lost in 1806 and upon the rebuilding of the army many new flags had to be issued (1808 pattern). Those pre-1806 flags that survived were re-issued along with the new pattern. The 1807 instructions called for two flags per musketeer battalion, as previously issued, but no flags for fusiliers or grenadiers. Grenadier formations were carrying flags by 1812 but fusiliers (with the exception of the fusiliers of guard grenadier units who received flags in 1814) did not get flags until after the wars in 1815. The first flag of each battalion was known as the 'Avancierfahne' and the second the 'Retirierfahne' (thus the 'Avancierfahne' of the first battalion was also the Liebfahne). By 1813 only the 'Avancierfahne' of each battalion was carried, the returned 'Retirierfahnen' often being issued to new units as their 'Avancierfahne'; thus many flags for different regiments were identical. Some of the changes of ownership have been noted in the following list.

June 1813 GRzuF=Garde-Regiment zu Fuss.

Type	Regiment	Flag	Ground colour	Centre	Embroidery	Cross	Remarks
11	1 GRzuF 1 Bttn.	LF	white	silver blue scroll	silver	none	yellow staff
11	1 GRzuF 11 Bttn.	RF	white	orange blue scroll	silver	none	yellow staff
11	2 GRzuF 1 Bttn.	RF	white	orange blue scroll	silver	none	yellow staff
11	2 GRzuF 11 Bttn. (ex Colberg Regiment, 1st Bttn.)	RF	black	orange blue scroll	gold	white straight	Colberg badge
11	1 1st Ost. Pruss. 1 Bttn.	LF	white	black white scroll	gold	none	gold eagle
1	1 1st Ost. Pruss. 11 Bttn.	RF	black	white black scroll	gold	none	white staff
I	2 1st Pomm. I Bttn. (1807 Nr. 8)	LF	white	black, white scroll	gold, inc. eagle	black wavy	white staff
I	2 1st Pomm. II Bttn.	RF	black	white, black scroll	gold	white straight	black staff
II	3 2nd Ost. Pruss. I Bttn.	LF	black	orange, blue scroll	gold	white straight	black staff
II	3 2nd Ost, Pruss. II Bttn.	RF	white	orange, blue scroll	gold	black straight	black staff
II	4 3rd Ost. Pruss. I Bttn.	LF	black	orange, blue scroll	gold	white straight	black staff
II	4 3rd Ost. Pruss. II Bttn.	RF	white	orange, blue scroll	gold	black straight	black staff
I	5 4th Ost. Pruss. I Bttn.	LF	white	white, white scroll	gold	orange wavy	red-brown staff
I	5 4th Ost. Pruss. II Bttn.	RF	orange	white, orange scroll	gold	white wavy	brown staff
I	6 1st West Pruss. I Bttn. (Pre. 1807 nr. 52)	LF	white	dark green, white scroll	silver	poppy red wavy	white staff
I	6 1st West Pruss. II Bttn.	RF	dark green	white, dark green scroll	silver	poppy red wavy	white staff
I	7 2nd West Pruss. I Bttn. (pre. 1807 Nr. 58)	LF	light yellow	light yellow, white scroll	silver	white straight	white staff
I	7 2nd West Pruss. II Bttn.	RF	light yellow	light yellow, light blue scroll	silver	light blue straight	white staff
II	8 1st Bradenburg I Bttn. (previously Leib. Inf. Reg.)	LF	black	orange, light blue scroll	gold	white straight	Colberg badge black staff
II	8 1st Bradenburg II Bttn.	RF	white	orange, light blue scroll	gold	black straight	Colberg badge white staff

Type	Regiment	Flag	Ground colour	Centre	Embroidery	Cross	Remarks
II	9 2nd Pomm. I Bttn.	LF	black	orange, light blue scroll	gold	white straight	Colberg badge black staff
(Previously Colberg Inf. Reg.)							
II	2nd Pomm. II Bttn.	RF	white	orange, light blue scoll	gold	black straight	Colberg badge black staff
(June 1813 2nd GRzuF Bttn. August 13 this became flag of 1st Bttn.)							
I	10 1st Schl. I Bttn.	LF	scarlet	white, scarlet scroll	gold	none	black staff
(Pre. 1807 Nr. 38)							
I	10 1st Schl. II Bttn.	RF	scarlet	white, scarlet scroll	gold	none	black staff
I	11 2nd Schl. I Bttn.	LF	cornflower blue	white, blue scroll	silver	none	white staff
(Pre. 1807 Nr. 33)							
I	11 2nd Schl. II Bttn.	RF	cornflower blue	white, blue scroll	silver	none	white staff

The numbering of the regiments altered in June 1813 because of the removal of the Guard Regiment zu Fuss from the line numbering. This had occupied position Nr. 8. Thus regiments 9 to 12 became 8 to 11. The 2nd Brandenburg regiment was raised to fill position Nr. 12. This regiment was issued with flags in 1815, along with the reserve regiments that were included in the line numbering at this time (numbers 13 onwards). This did not take place until after Waterloo and is thus outside the scope of this book.

Grenadier formation flags.

	Type	Regiment	Flag	Ground colour	Centre	Embroidery	Cross	Remarks
1807 Nr. 2	I	1st Ost. Pruss. Gren. Bttn.	RF	black	white black scroll	gold	none	white staff
		(In 1814 the II Bttn. Kaiser-Alexander-Garde-Grenadier-Regt.)						
	I	West Pruss. Gren. Bttn.	RF	lt. yellow	lt. yellow blue scroll	silver	lt. blue straight	white staff
		(In 1814 the II Bttn. Kaiser-Franz-Garde-Grenadier-Regt.)						
1807 Nr. 33	I	Schles. Gren. Bttn.	RF	cornflower blue	white blue scroll	silver	none	white staff
		(In 1814 Kaiser-Franz-Garde-Grenadier-Regt. Fusilier Bttn.)						
	II	Leib-Gren. Bttn.	RF	white	orange blue scroll	gold	black straight	Colberg badge black staff
		(In 1814 1st Bttn. Kaiser-Alexander-Garde-Grenadier-Regt.)						
	II	2nd Ost. Pruss. Gren. Bttn.	RF	white	orange blue scroll	gold	black straight	black staff
		(In 1814 Kaiser-Alexander-Garde-Grenadier-Regt. Fusilier Bttn.)						
1807 Nr. 8	I	Pomm. Gren. Bttn.	RF	black	white black scroll	gold	white wavy	white staff
		(In 1814 I Bttn. Kaiser-Franz-Garde-Grenadier-Regt.)						

Cavalry standards also dated from the time of Frederick the Great. In the reorganisation of 1807 only Dragoon and Kurassier regiments were to carry standards. The Hussars did not again have standards until after the end of the conflict in 1815. Those allowed standards at first had one to a squadron (that of the first squadron being the Leib-standard) but after 1811 only the first squadron standard was carried on campaign. Two patterns existed: Kurassier (square) and

Dragoon (swallow-tailed). The titles did not refer to the designation of the bearing unit but the regiment to which the colour had belonged before the reorganisation. Thus the 2nd Kurassier regiment bore a Dragoon pattern standard which had belonged to the old Dragoon Regiment Auer.

Some examples of these standards are as follows:—

Dragoons Rgt. Nr. 1. Dragoon pattern. Red ground with large black, curved-sided cross. Light blue centre with gold embroidery. (Ex 7th regiment of Dragoons.)

Dragoon regiment Nr. 2. Dragoon pattern. Red with light blue cross. White centre, gold embroidery. (Ex Dragoon Rgt. Auer, also pattern for 2nd Kurassier.)

Dragoon Rgt. Nr. 3. Dragoon pattern. Red, black cross. Silver and white mixed centre, gold embroidery.

Dragoon Rgt. Nr. 5. Dragoon pattern. Black with white/silver centre, gold embroidery.

Kurassier Rgt. Nr. 2. Dragoon pattern. Red with light blue cross. White centre, gold embroidery.

Garde du Corps. Kurassier pattern. White with orange centre and backgrounds to corner medallions. Silver embroidery.

101 Infantry, 1808-15 flag showing form of wavy cross. Shown here as the Leibfahne of the first muster (pre-1808 pattern flags) for regiment No. 5, the 1st East Prussian.

102 Guard Grenadier regiment No. 2, 1814. This flag, like others of the first muster that were issued in 1813, is on the same pattern as other first muster flags but has the corner monograms of the second muster type. Shown here is the form of the straight-sided cross.

103 Flag of the second muster. Retirierfahne of Colberg infantry regiments. Design the same (with appropriate cross form) for all regiments except Colberg badge only carried by those units as indicated in list for 1813.

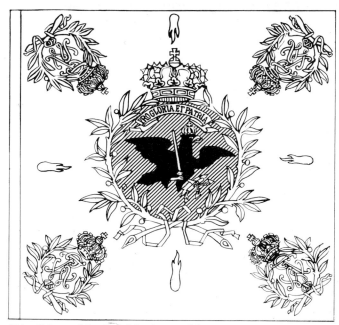

107   Infantry flag staff point, 1813.

104   Colour of 1st Guard Regiment of foot, 1813. Note this flag has features of both first and second muster flags. Shape and general design is like that of the second muster but centre is of the first muster type. Both battalions of the 1st Guard regiment and the first battalion of the 2nd Guard regiment carried flags of this pattern.

106   Kurassier standard.

105   'Dragoon' standard.

108 Landwehr flag. Battalion Sagun. Buff cloth with all designs in gold.

109 Flag of one of the volunteer and landwehr units raised in 1813. The flag of the Hans-Legion in Lubeck. White cloth with red cross; all other designs, staff head and fringes in gold.

Russia

Changes of design in Russian flags and standards took place in 1800, 1803 and 1813. Old patterns were not always withdrawn however, and therefore some regiments still carried the 1800 pattern after 1803, and others the 1803 after 1813. In 1803 each infantry regiment has one 'white' flag (equivalent to the Leibfahne) and one 'coloured' flag per battalion or squadron. Previous to this each company could have carried a flag. In 1813 the 'white' flag was discontinued; each battalion now only had one flag and there were only three standards to each cavalry regiment.

The 1800 line infantry flag was as illustration '110' and measured 140cm. by 140cm. The 'white' flag had a white background with corner rays of a colour determined by the area (Inspection) in which the town from which they took their name was located, as follows:—

Inspections	White colour corners	Company colour background, corners	Embroidery	Upright cross
Brest Litovsk, Lithuania, Livonia, Smolensk	half black, half red	black, red	silver	none
Caucasus, Dniester, Crimea, Ukraine	half yellow	yellow, white	gold	yes
Finland, Moscow	half black, half lt. blue	lt. blue, black	gold	none
St. Petersburg	half deep pink	deep pink, white	gold	yes
Orenburg, Siberia	half yellow, half green	yellow, green	gold	none

Individual regiments within the Inspection were distinguished by the colour of the staff—brown, yellow, black or white. The central circle for all regiments was orange with a black double eagle crowned and armed gold. Thunderbolts and lightning gold. The eagle always pointed towards the upper fly corner on both sides. Ribbons were light blue and bore the inscription shown in illustration '110' on one side, and that shown in illustration '112' on the other. Laurels were tied in light blue ribbon, and were gold.

The corner devices were in the regimental metal colour. Some flags had a white upright maltese cross on the field as indicated in the above table. This took up approximately one fifth of the height of the edge and tapered towards the centre like the corner rays

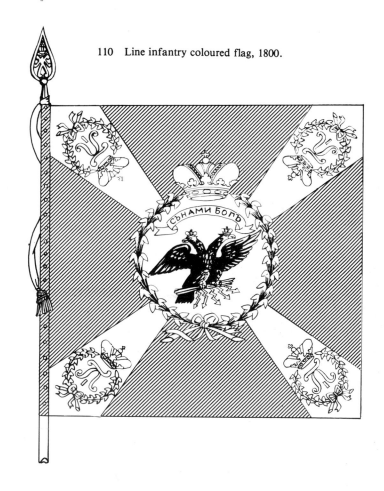

110   Line infantry coloured flag, 1800.

Battle honours were awarded in the form of inscriptions on a second blue scroll below the eagle. Cords and tassels were silver, orange and black. The flags of the three guard infantry regiments of the time were of a similar design to those of the line. The flags were the same for all three regiments with the flag staffs in a distinctive colour. These were: Ismailovsky, white; Semenovsky, black; Preobrajensky, straw yellow for coloured and brown for 'white' colour.

The flags themselves were as illustration '112'; the 'coloured' colour having a red background with white corners and white upright cross. The 'white' colour had a white background with red half corners. All other colours were as the line infantry flags with the corner devices in gold.

The 1803-pattern flags had a new style eagle, laurel wreath and corner monogram. The light blue scroll above the eagle also disappeared as did the corner rays on the 'white' colour, the background now being completely white with the devices as on the 'coloured' colours. The flag staffs were no longer used as a form of regimental distinction, all now being black, and topped with a new style pike head. The colours of the various Inspections were revised as per the following table:—

Inspection	Background	Inspection	Background
Brest Litévsk	Deep yellow	Livonia	Turquoise
Dniester	Lilac	Moscow	Orange
Caucasus	Blue	St. Petersburg	Black
Crimea	Light brown	Orenburg	Buff
Finland	Yellow	Siberia	Grey
Kiev	Deep pink	Smolensk	White
Lithuania	Pale green	Ukraine	Pale pink

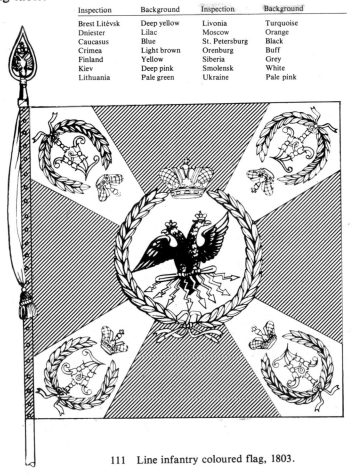

111   Line infantry coloured flag, 1803.

Corner rays were in all cases white with the exception of St. Petersburg which had red. As before, the central circle was orange with a black eagle and gold details. After 1807 the 'Inspection' system was no longer used, and flags issued from that year to newly raised regiments did not follow a system as far as colours were concerned. A few known examples of flags issued during this period (1807-13) are listed below:—

Name of Regiment	Background	Corners
Belostoksky Musketeers	blue	red
Pernovsky	green	white
Azovsky	pale pink	chocolate
Fanagorisky Grenadiers	pale pink	green
Odessky Infantry	yellow	half black, half white
Grouzinsky Grenadiers	purple	deep orange
Permsky Infantry	brown	green

Units that had a particularly distinguished record were honoured with a 'colour of St. George'. This was the ordinary standard but with an inscription around the border describing the action for which the award was made and the date of it being given. The pike staff was replaced with one bearing a white enamelled cross, and the cords were orange with three black stripes. Tassels were silver with black tracery. The flags of the Pernovsky Musketeers and Fanagorisky Grenadiers as described in the preceding table were colours of St. George.

112   Guard 'white' flag, 1800.

In 1813 all new flags issued to the line infantry were green with white corners. Design was that shown in illustration '113' but with relevant border inscriptions only carried by those regiments entitled to colours of St. George. The examples below are of some of the regiments that are known to have been issued with the new style flags and all were entitled to colours of St. George:—
Grenadiers of Count Arkcheev, Fiajsky Infantry, Kamchatsky Infantry, Pernovsky Grenadiers and Keksholmsky Grenadiers.

The Guard Infantry were issued in 1813 with flags of the same pattern as those of that date for the line infantry, but all with yellow backgrounds and corners of individuals colours:—

Regiment	Colours	Regiment	Colours
Preobrajensky	half red, half white	Findlandsky	half green, half black
Semenovsky	half light blue, half white	Grenadiers	half light blue, half black
Isamailovsky	white	Litovsky	half red, half black
Pavlovsky	half white, half black	Yegersky	half green, half white

113   Guard colour of Preobrajensky Guards, 1813.

All were colours of St. George.
As before, the black eagle was on a central orange circle but now in a different form. The breast shield bore St. George in silver armour on a white horse, killing a green dragon, against a red background.

The line cavalry, at the beginning of the Napoleonic wars, carried the standards of 1797. The Curassier's were as illustration '115', one 'white' and four 'coloured' were carried by each regiment. As with the infantry flags the field of the white standards was white. The backgrounds to the corner monograms were in a regimental colour, and the laurels, monograms, borders, fringes and foliage pattern were all in the metal colour indicated for each individual regiment. The eagle was black with beak, claws, thunderbolts and lightning always gold, as were the rays behind the silver cross. The distinctions for each regiment were as follows:—

Regiment	Coloured colour background, corner device	White colour corner device	Metal
Emperor's Leib-Cuirassiers	lt. blue, white	lt. blue	silver
Empress's Leib-Cuirassiers	deep pink, lt. blue	deep pink	silver
Cuirassiers of the Military Order	black, white	black	gold
Gloukhovsky	beige, orange	beige	silver
Ekaterinoslavsky	orange, lt. blue	lt. blue	silver
Kanzansky	green, red	red	gold
Kievsky	deep yellow, purple	deep purple	silver
Malorossiisky	purple, lt. green	purple	gold
Nejinsky	red, white	white	gold
Rejinsky	beige, lt. blue	lt. blue	gold
Rlazansky	lt. blue, white	lt. blue	gold
Sofiisky	orange, lt. blue	lt. blue	gold
Starodoubovsky	dark green, white	dark green	silver
Kharkhovsky	pink, puce	puce	silver
Tchernigosvsky	yellow, puce	puce	silver
Iambourgsky	green, white	green	gold
Neplouieva	deep pink, dark grey	dark grey	silver
Frideritsia	mauve, orange	mauve	gold
Zorna	yellow, red	yellow	gold

114 Dragoon standard, 1797.

115 Curassier standard, 1797.

Cavalry standards were usually made of heavy brocaded material. The Dragoon regiments carried standards of the pattern shown in illustration '114' (with the exception of three regiments that were formed from Cuirassier regiments and continued to carry Cuirassier-style standards). The centre circle was orange with the black double eagle. Breast shield bore the St. George motif as described for the 1813 infantry flags, in the same colours. Crowns, beak, feet, orb, sceptre and order chain were all in gold. The wreath was green. The regimental distinctions were as follows:—

Regiment	Coloured standard background, corners	White standard corners	Metal
Astrakhansky	yellow, lt. blue	half lt. blue, half yellow	silver
Hastatova	half red, half white, dark blue	half red. half dark blue	silver
Ingermanland	deep pink, white	deep pink	gold
Irkutsky	lt. blue, red	half red, half lt. blue	gold
Kargopolsky	lt. blue, white	lt. blue	silver
Moskovsky	orange, lt. blue	half orange, half lt. blue	silver
Narvsky	purple, white	purple	silver
Nijegorodsky	half lt. orange, half white, black	half lt. orange, half black	silver
Orenbursky	red, white	red	gold
Pskovsky	yellow, white	yellow	gold
Rostovsky	blue, white	blue	silver
Sversky	orange, black	half black, half orange	silver
Shreidersa	half white, half dark green, white	half white, half dark green	gold
Sibirsky	red, green	half red, half green	silver
Smolensky	orange, purple	half orange, half purple	gold
St. Petersburg	green, white	green	gold
Taganrogaky	red, yellow	half yellow, half red	gold

In 1803 the pattern of standard was made the same for all branches of the arm, as illustrated in figure '116'. The coloured standards were green with white corner devices for all regiments, the white standard being white with green corner devices. All designs, including the eagle, were now in gold. Some of the regiments that were known to have received these new colours are listed below. Borisoglebsky Dragoons, Peregaslavsky Dragoons, Jitomirsky Dragoons, Tchernigosvsky Dragoons, Tiraspolsky Dragoons, Starodoubovsky Dragoons, Astrakhansky Cuirassiers and Pavlogradsky Hussars. Colours of St. George were awarded with the same distinctions as described for the infantry, the inscriptions replacing the foliage of the border. The Starodoubovsky and Tchernigosvsky Dragoons and the Pavlogradsky Hussars in the above list had colours of St. George.

The Cossacks and other irregular cavalry units also carried flags but the designs seemed to be very much to the personal taste of the commander. Some units were known to have carried standards of the 1797 dragoon pattern in colours of their own choice. Other patterns included many religious symbols and inscriptions, some units having several standards of various designs and colour schemes.

The guard cavalry standards followed the same general pattern as those for the line but inscriptions replaced the foliage in the borders.

Up to 1807 the Horse Guards carried one white and nine coloured standards of the pattern shown in illustration '117'. The other side was the same but with the eagle again near the staff. The 'white' standard had a white background with pink corner decorations. Eagle and rays behind cross were gold. Corner laurels and monogram, cross, outlines to borders, inscriptions and fringes were all silver. Pike head was gilt, cords and tassels silver with orange and black tracery. Pike was green with fluting picked out in gold. Coloured standards were the same except that the main background colour was deep pink and the corner devices buff. This design was replaced in 1807 by one white and five green standards of a new pattern as shown in illustration '118'. Ribbon was light blue with honour inscription. Corner medallions were buff. All embroidery was gold. Staffs were green with gold lined fluting. Cords, tassels and ribbons were silver with mixed black and orange lines. Guard Dragoons were issued with similar standards in 1809 but without the honour ribbons.

117   Horse Guards before 1807.

116   Cavalry standard, 1803.

118   Horse Guards, 1807.

Saxony

In 1802 new flags were issued to the thirteen infantry regiments (twelve line one guard) of the Saxon army. Each regiment had a white Leib flag and a regimental flag in the facing colour of the unit. Borders of the flags were also to a regimental pattern. The regiments and their colours at this time were as follows:-

Regiment	Border	Regimental flag colour
Leibgrenadier Guard	Leibfahne red and green, Bataillonsfahne blue and silver	yellow
Kurfurst (Konig) Sanger	red/yellow/white with green leaves	orange/red
Prinz Anton Prinz Clemens	blue and yellow	deep sky blue
Prinz Maximilian	yellow/orange with green leaves	yellow
Nostitv (v Thimmel)	orange/silver with gold leaves	yellow
Prinz Friedrich August	Black, green leaves, oak leaves, yellow 'flowers'	green
Von Low	same as above but with white 'flowers'	green
Prinz Xaver	yellow/blue	light blue
Von Ryssel	blue/silver	light blue
Von Rechten	orange red/silver with gold clover leaves	crimson
Von Niesemeuschel	as above but clover leaves also silver	crimson

These flags for reasons of economy had been painted and they did not stand up well to the conditions of campaign. In 1807 new flags were ordered. These were to be of the same general pattern as the old colours but with differences to the monograms and crests. The regiments Sanger, Nostitz, Prinz Xaver and Von Ryssel had been disbanded. These new flags were embroidered, and because of delays and the difficulty of communications these were not presented to the regiments until 1811.

Saxon infantry regiments in 1811 each had two battalions and each battalion carried a flag, the Leibfahne for the first battalion and the Ordinarfahne for the second. The general design was similar for all regiments but each had its own border design and a different background colour for the ordinary flag. Sizes varied slightly from 142cm. to 151cm. by 143cm. For both Leibfahne and Ordinarfahne the design was the same, the background being white for the Leibfahne. The shield design was in outline only, the background colour showing through. On the reverse side the coat of arms, as shown in the illustration, replaced the shield and foliage, and the corner shields bearing the arms of Saxony were replaced by gold outline shields bearing the letters "RS". The colours common to all regiments were thus:— Gold crown outline to shield and

119 Basic pattern of Saxon Infantry flags (here shown with border of regiment Konig). 119b is central design for other side in the same scale.

monogram design, gold orders below shield, green and red gems on crown. Green laurels ferns and drapery. Corner shields black and yellow bands with green diagonal (Arms of Saxony). Obverse: The Arms of Saxony with drapery, orders and crown as already described. Mantle red, lined ermine (white with black darts). Gold cords to mantle and gold "RS" corner shields as already described.

The staff was 170cm. long and coloured the same as the background to the ordinary flag with the exception of the Leibfahne of the Leib-Grenadiers The regimental distinctions were as follows:—

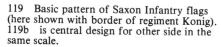

rders of infantry flags.

Name of Regiment	Border design and colours	Background colour of ordinary flag	
Konig	F. Orange/red background, dark red outer border, yellow inner border, dark red and yellow alternate loops.	Orange red	d
Niesemeuschel	C. Crimson background, silver design.	Crimson	
Prinz Anton	D. Sky blue background, gold design.	Sky blue	e
Low	G. Green background, silver design and border	Green	
Prinz Maximilian	B. Yellow background, orange loops and border, green intervening leaves.	Yellow	
Rechten	C. Crimson background, gold design	Crimson	f
Prinz Friedrich August	G. Green background, brown oak leaves and border. Yellow diamond designs	Green	
Steindel (Prinz Clemens)	D. Sky blue background, silver design	Sky blue	g

The Leib Grenadiers had different border designs for the Leib and ordinary flags. That of the Leibfahne was as design 'E' and had a red ribbon on a white background with a green design overall. The ordinarfahne was yellow and the background to the border was the same colour. The design was as fig. 'A', having a blue ribbon with narrow blue flanking lines. The overall leaf design was white.

In the Saxon cavalry a regiment consisted of four squadrons, each of which had a standard. The Hussars did not have standards.

The designs of the standards were as follows:—

Gardes du Corps. 52cm by 64cm on a staff 170cm long. The standard for this unit was as illustration '121A'. The field was white as was the background to the border. Outline and loop decoration within the border were gold and the crosses silver. Coat of arms was as described for the infantry flags. The fringe, cords and tassels were sky blue and gold mixed. The obverse was similar but the coat of arms was replaced by the laurels and crowned monogram as shown for the standards of the other cavalry regiments. Laurels were green with brown stems, monogram and crown gold, The latter with red and green gems. Staff was brown and pike head gilt.

Cuirassiers de Zastrow. Size similar to that of Garde du Corps standard. The design was as per illustration '122'. Field was white as was the background to the border. Outline and loops and dots in the border design were yellow. Foliage between loops was green. Coat of arms was as the infantry flags and monogram the same as for the Gardes du Corps. The fringe was red and white mixed. Cords and tassels were yellow and silver.

Leib-Cuirassiers. Standard the same as that for the Cuirassiers de Zastrow but the border pattern was as illustration '124B'. Outlines to border were yellow with the rest of the design in crimson on a white background. Fringe, cords and tassels were crimson and white mixed.

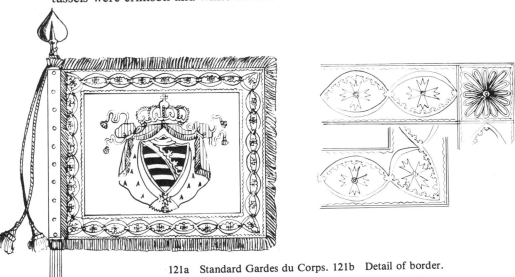

121a Standard Gardes du Corps. 121b Detail of border.

The four Chevaux-Leger regiments had standards of a common pattern with different borders. The first (Leib) squadron of each regiment carried the Leib-standard which had a white background, and the other squadrons had standards with crimson backgrounds to the centre panels. Fringes, cords and tassels were crimson and white. The pattern was the same as that shown for the Cuirassiers de Zastrow.

The regiment Prinz Clemens. Border design as per illustration '123B'. White background, border and main design green with the ovals violet.

The regiment Prinz Albrecht. Border design as per illustration '123D'. White background, green outlines and leaves, brown acorns.

The regiment Prinz Johann. Border design as per illustration '123A'. White background with yellow outlines. Palm leaves green with jagged design and diamond shapes in black.

Regiment de Polentz. Border design as per illustration '123C'. Background white with outlines in gold. All other parts of the design were sky blue highlighted in gold as shown. To differentiate between the squadrons of each regiment cravats were attached to the pike head of each standard in a squadron colour. These were 1st (Leib) squadron white, 2nd squadron red, 3rd squadron blue and 4th squadron yellow.

After the general defection of Saxony in 1813 many Landwehr and volunteer units were formed. These often carried flags made by the troops' womenfolk and were generally white with a green Landwehr cross (or sometimes vice versa), often with a town crest and a motto.

122 Pattern of standard for cavalry regiment other than Gardes du Corps (here shown with border of Cuirassiers de Zastrow).

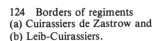

124 Borders of regiments
(a) Cuirassiers de Zastrow and
(b) Leib-Cuirassiers.

123 Borders of cavalry regiments.

Spain

Each battalion of infantry had two flags, a King's and a Battalion colour. These were usually carried by junior officers on a brown or black staff with a plain white metal pike head. Spanish flags were embroidered and it seems they had the designs outlined with piping of black and/or gold before the solid colours were embroidered in. This piping showed on the finished flag as a thin black outline to the designs.

The King's colour measured approximately 120cm by 150cm. and was white. In the centre were the crowned Arms of Spain surrounded by an ornate chain. The whole device was very large, the tip of the crown and the bottom of the chain almost touching the edges of the flag. In the corners were badges of regimental significance (either placed upright or at an angle pointing outwards), the King's badge, or the badge of the province or town named in their title.

The battalion colour was of a similar size to the King's colour, and was also white. The cross of ragged staffs was red with the badges in the corners as for the King's colour. These badges were either in gold embroidery or often in black outline only.

125 Battalion colour.

Cavalry standards were carried by junior officers in the dragoon and heavy cavalry regiments. These standards seem to have been of a universal pattern. The field colour was crimson and on one side were the Arms of Spain contained within a scrollwork frame of gold embroidery. Gold fringes were on three sides, and often a small badge of regimental significance (e.g. Fleur de Lys, grenade, etc,) in gold in each corner. Cravat was usually crimson.

Sweden

The Swedish infantry carried one 'Lifkompani' flag plus a 'Kompanifana' for each other company. The flags measured approximately 170cm by 190cm. They were carried on white painted staffs tipped with gilt spear points pierced to show the sovereign's initials. The 'Lifkompani' flag or 'Liffana' was white with the Royal Swedish crest in the centre. In the upper canton next to the staff was a small provincial badge. The 'Kompanifana' were in provincial colours with the relevant badge in the centre on both sides. This badge was within a laurel prior to 1792, but borne on a crowned shield bordered with laurel after this date. Cravats were in provincial colours. The 'Lifregementets' or household troops had a Liffana like those described above but their 'Kompanifana' were also white and bore a crowned monogram within a palm wreath on both sides.

The cavalry bore either a swallow-tailed (Dragoon) or square standard according to the type of the regiment. The swallow-tailed standard measured 92cm high by 108cm to the tip of the tail. As with the infantry, one white 'Liffa' was carried per regiment plus one 'Kompanistandar' per subsequent company. The designs followed those of the infantry flags, but the 'Kompanistandar' carried the provincial badge on one side only, being replaced by the sovereign's monogram within palm leaves on the other. Lances were white for the Liffa and in provincial colours for the 'Kompanistandar'. Standards were fringed and had cravats in provincial colours attached. The square cavalry standards measured 67cm by 65cm and followed the same design as the 'Dragoon' standards.

Kompanifana Skaraborg Infantry regiment, model. Black over yellow field. Central shield and yellow with lion counter-changed. Gold and frame. There should be two silver six-stars in the black portion of the centre shield these are absent on a surviving relic of this

127 Kompanifana Helsinge Infantry regiment, 1766 model. Black and white field with black central shield surrounded by gold foliage and topped by gold crown. Gold goat had red hooves and horns. White staff.

128 Kompanifana Vastgota-Dals regiment, 1800. White field. Black and yellow centre badge as 127. Gold frame, crown and wreath. White staff.

129 Kompanifana Vastgota Infantry regiment, 1808. White and light blue field. Centre crest black and yellow with gold lion and silver stars. Crown gold, laurel wreath green. White staff.

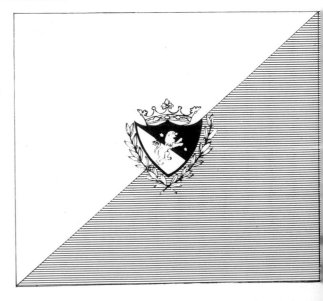

Warsaw

In 1807 eagles were issued to the regiments of the newly defined Grand Duchy of Warsaw. Officially one eagle was to be issued to each regiment, to be carried by the first battalion, each subsequent battalion having a flag but no eagle. However it seems that some battalions other than the first received eagles in most regiments. The eagles were usually carried by a junior officer or sometimes a senior NCO. Design of flags and even of eagles varied as did the size of the flag. The following list sets out, regiment by regiment, the details of the flags and eagles where known.

1st regiment of line infantry:—
Eagle . . . .White metal with gold crown.
White metal base with gold lettering,
on the front PULK Iszy/PIECHOTY
on the rear WOYSKO/POLSKIE
The flag was crimson and measured 55cm square. The central eagle was white and below this was the inscription in yellow:—PULK PIERWSZY/PIECHOTY. Both sides the same.

The above flag was probably issued to replace that taken by the Russians in 1812. The flag was in a very ragged state when captured and was described as a white flag 95cm wide by 80cm deep. In the centre was a cock (or eagle) with the inscription on one side LEGION POLONAISE and on the other REPUBLIQUE FRANCAISE. The flag had a gold fringe and the staff was tipped with an eagle exactly like that described for the crimson flag. This white flag was probably a regimental heirloom dating from an earlier period.

2nd regiment of line infantry:—
Flag 48cm by 50cm of crimson material. Both sides were the same and bore the white eagle in the centre (actually further toward the fly) with the inscriptions in white . . . . above: LEGIA.1., and below the eagle, PULK 2yc PIEHOTY. The flag was edged with a silver fringe on three sides.

4th regiment of line infantry:—
Two flags are known for this regiment. The first was crimson and had the white Polish eagle in the centre. Above was the legend:—
'Gdy sie chie bronic nie
in nych ciemiezyc
haslem Polaka zginac, lub zwyciezyc'.
This, roughly translated means, "To defend ourselves, and not to oppress others, the slogan of the Polish is to die or vanquish".
The second flag was also crimson and measured 42cm by 51cm. The centre bore the white Polish eagle with beak and claws worked in gold wire. The words PUTK 4 were below the eagle also in gold wire. The opposite side was light blue and bore the same design as the crimson side but with the addition of an inscription in small lettering just inside and parallel to the fly edge.
This inscription read . . . 'Svte reka Zofic Potocki Zony Pierwszego Polkownika

Regimenta'.

This means . . . "Sewn and made by the hand of Sofia Potocki wife of the First Colonel of the regiment". The flag had a silver fringe.

5th regiment of line infantry:—

This regiment had an uncrowned eagle with, on its silver base to the front, WOYSKO POLSKIE and on the rear PULK . . . (No. of regiment) PIECHOTY in yellow metal and was carried on a staff 224cm long. Details of the flag are unknown but it was crimson with the usual white eagle in the centre. Above the eagle was an inscription, probably a unit designation. The flag had a silver fringe.

6th regiment of line infantry:—

Flag was 54cm by 50cm and crimson. White eagle with orb, sceptre and crown in gold wire. In yellow lettering were the inscriptions WOYSKO POLSKIE above the eagle, and PULK SZUSTY below. The flag had a silver fringe.

8th regiment of line infantry:—

Crimson flag 42cm square. On both sides a white laurel wreath tied at the base with a blue ribbon. On one side within the wreath the words PULK 8^{SZY}/PIECHOTY and on the other side the words BATALION Ie. The lettering was in black embroidery. Silver fringe.

10th regiment of line infantry:—

Silver eagle with gold crown. Silver base with lettering in gold:—PULK 10ty PIECHOTY on the front and WOYSKO POLSKIE on the back. No flag is known but a white cravat 53cm long and 14cm wide was attached to the 292cm long staff. A design of oak leaves in gold ran along the ends of the cravat which were finished with gold fringes.

11th regiment of line infantry:—

Silver eagle without crown. Base same as for the 10th regiment except the number 11sy was substituted for 10ty. Again no flag is known but a white gold-ringed cravat like that of the 10th regiment (but without the oak leaf embroidery) was attached to the staff.

13th regiment of line infantry:—

Silver eagle with gold crown. Base as 10th regiment but 13 substituted for 10. White cravat 62cm long with a border of stars and a fringe in silver. This regiment also had a second eagle but without a crown. The inscriptions on the base were the same but in reverse positions i.e. WOYSKO POLSKIE on the front face. With this eagle was a flag of individual design. The flag was white and the devices were painted. Within the edges of the flag was a silver border and within this a further border of gold laurel leaves. In the centre was a seated figure in blue and white robes, face and hair natural. She held in one hand a golden eagle on a staff and in the other a silver oval shield bearing the letters:—S.P.Q.R. in gold. Behind the figure was an anchor and at her feet a wolf suckling the twins, all in natural colours. Around this motif was a gold flat-cornered frame. Above this frame was a gold scroll with, in silver, the word PULK. There was space left on the scroll for the regimental number but this was missing. This flag had silver fringes on all four sides and two cords and tassels in gold hung from the staff-head. The other side was the same but the central motif was reversed left to right so that the figure always faced the fly.

14th regiment of line infantry:—

Silver uncrowned eagle. Plinth as 10th regiment with 14 in place of 10. Flag 56cm by 77cm high. One side blue with the white eagle. Above the eagle the lettering POLK 14sty and below the eagle BATTALION 1szy all in white. The other side was crimson with the lettering POLK 14sty/PIECHOTY LINIONEY/BATTon 1szy again all in white.

17the regiment of line infantry:—

Flag crimson, measuring 52cm by 46cm. On one side was a white outline circle enclosing the words POLK 17/IMIENIA/ZAMOYSKICH. At an angle in each corner pointing towards the centre was a white grenade. On the other side was the white eagle on crimson.

In most cases the eagle on the flags was embroidered in white silk. Sometimes the legs, beak and crown were added in gold wire and often the orb and sceptre were in silver wire.

Cavalry standards were much like the infantry flags but the eagles were of different pattern and sometimes made of wood. The plinth was a different shape. The standard of the 1st Chasseurs à cheval measured 61cm square. The cloth was crimson and all embroidery in silver, comprising the usual eagle with the inscriptions LEGIAI. above, and I PULK LEKKI IAZDV below. Both sides were the same. Cords, tassels and fringes were silver. The eagle atop the staff was silver with a silver crown. The plinth was also silver with a dark blue insert on which in gold lettering were the words POLSKIE on the front face and WOYSKO on the rear. The 15th Lancers had a crimson standard 57cm by 55cm. The silver eagle was on both sides with the yellow number XV in the lower fly corner in each case. Cords, tassels and fringes were silver.

130 4th line infantry.

131 6th line infantry.

132 8th line infantry.

133   14th line infantry.

134   Standard 1st Chasseurs.

135   13th line infantry.

Westphalia

The first flags issued to the Westphalian troops in 1808 followed the French design. Carried by a senior NCO, they measured between 85cm and 90cm square. Infantry were entitled to carry one flag per battalion. The first (1808) issue was blue with a white central lozenge. Corner wreaths and other decorations were in gold and similar to the French pattern except that a 'JN' monogram was within the wreath in two of the corners on each side. The inscriptions were in French and were on the one side:—
LE ROI/DE WESTPHALIE/AU/(number of regiment)/REGIMENT/D'INFANTERIE/DE LIGNE

and on the other:—

VALEUR/ET/DISCIPLINE/(number of battalion)/BATAILLON

Staffs were 170cm long and painted blue; the plain spear head was white metal.

In 1810 flags of a similar design but with German inscriptions were issued. These were as follows:—

DER/KONIG/VON/WESPHALIEN/(number of regiment) LINIEN INFANTERIE/REGIMENT

and on the other side:—

TAPFERKEIT/UND/GUTES BETRAGEN/(number of battalion)/BATAILLON

The 'JN' monograms were replaced on this issue of flags with a six-point star. In 1813 new flags were less ornate, the laurel surround to the central lozenge having disappeared. The German inscriptions were now in 'Gothic' lettering, the wording being similar to that of the 1809 flags. The corner wreaths now enclosed the regimental number.

The Guard infantry flags followed similar design to those of the line infantry. The 1808 pattern was blue with a white central lozenge. Inscriptions were, on the one side:—

LE ROI/DE WESTPHALIE/AU BATAILLON DE/GRENADIERS GARDES

and on the other side:—

VALEUR/ET DISCIPLINE

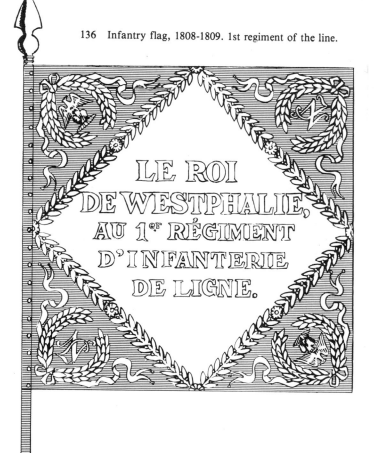

136   Infantry flag, 1808-1809. 1st regiment of the line.

Corner wreaths were empty. Flag staff was white and bore a gilt spearpoint with 'JN' inscribed therein. In 1812 a flag of new pattern was issued to the guards. This was blue with a broad diagonal cross in white. On one side in Gothic text was the inscription:—

Der Konig/von Westphalien/dem Bataillon/Grenadier-Garde

On the four blue triangles there were gold eagles. The other side was also blue with a broad white cross. The centre bore a coat of arms in full colours. The blue triangles were occupied by golden 'HN' monograms. The flag had a gold fringe and was carried on a blue and white spiral-painted staff. The spear point was pierced in a 'JN' design.

Cavalry standards in 1808 were blue with a broad white diagonal cross. One side bore the 'HN' monogram in gold, the other the coat of arms as described for the 1812 Guard flag. These standards were 60cm square and bore French inscriptions, these being replaced in 1812 by German. The 1812 standard for the Grade Du Corps was blue with a broad white diagonal cross. On one side were the four eagles and inscription:—

DER KONIG/VON WESTPHALIEN/AN SEINE/LEIRGARDE ZU PFERDE

The other side bore the crest and 'HN' monogram exactly like that of the Grenadier Guard flag. The standard was fringed in gold. New standards decreed in 1813 were vertically divided blue (next to staff) and white, with golden German gothic inscriptions.

In 1807 Napoleon raised for French service a Westphalien regiment. The flag of this unit was of the French 1804 pattern but considerably larger measuring 164cm square. Both sides were similar with the inscription on one side:—

L'EMPEREUR/DES FRANCAIS/AU REGIMENT/DE WESTPHALIE

and on the other:—

VALEUR/ET DISCIPLINE/ler BATAILLON (see illustration in French section)

137   Infantry flag, 1809. 7th regiment of the line.

138   Infantry flag, 1813. 2nd regiment of the line.

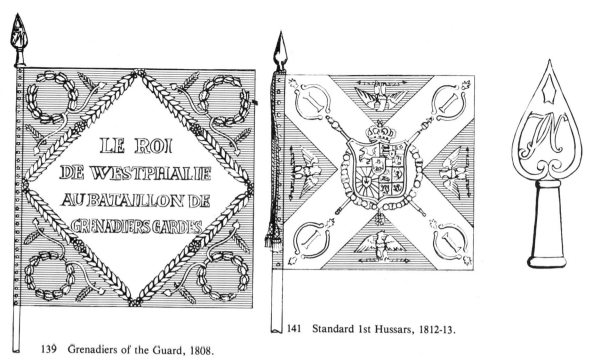

139 Grenadiers of the Guard, 1808.

141 Standard 1st Hussars, 1812-13.

140 Grenadiers of the Guard, 1812.

Wurttemberg

The 1811 pattern Wurttemberg infantry flag measured 132cm by 118cm, on a 308cm-long staff. The staff was painted black to a point approximately halfway down, with the lower portion brown. The pike head was gilt. Each regiment had two flags of exactly the same design except the regiment No 6 KRONPRINZ which had four. The design was the same for all regiments, the distinction between them being shown by the background colour as follows:—

	Regiment	Colour of background
1	PRINZ PAUL	lemon yellow
2	PRINZ WILHELM	red
3		blue
4	FRANQUEMONT	pink
5	PRINZ FRIEDRICH	sky blue
6	KRONPRINZ	quarterly blue and white
7		quarterly blue and red
8		quarterly blue and yellow
9		dark blue

All had gold fringes.

142   Design for all flags; colours only indicated regiment.

According to descriptions in 1814, the 7th regiment then had two blue and yellow quartered flags (1st battalion) and two yellow flags (2nd battalion), all of the same pattern. The 8th regiment had two blue and red quartered flags (1st battalion) and two red flags (2nd battalion). It seems the flags of the 7th and 8th regiments were swapped. All other regiments had four flags of the old pattern with the exception of the 9th regiment which only had two.

Of the Wurttemberg cavalry only the two Chevau-Legers regiments carried standards in 1811. The standards of the two squadrons of the 1st Chevau-Legers (one to each squadron) were yellow and of the same pattern as the infantry flags. Those of the 2nd regiment were red. All had gold fringes and the 'FR' pierced tip as for the infantry.

Wurzburg

A regiment of two battalions was raised by the Grand Duke Ferdinand in 1805. Four flags were presented to the regiment in 1806 when it became the first regiment of the Confederation of the Rhine. The flags were all of the same design and measured 160cm by 120cm. The field was lemon yellow and was surrounded by a border of red, white and blue triangles. On one side was a red

143   Infantry flag. For other side see colour section.

letter 'F' beneath a golden crown, both surrounded by green laurel branches tied with red ribbon. The other side bore as its central device a combined coat of arms within a mantle (see colour plate). The flag was carried on a red and white spiral-painted staff. In 1812 the regiment was four battalions strong with a fifth acting as a depot battalion. Two flags exist for this depot battalion, both the same, and of a generally similar design to the others but with the following differences:— The monogram now read 'FII', and the borders consisted of white and yellow flames. The coat of arms was simplified and consisted of the quartered arms of Wurzburg and Tuscany. In 1814 the regiment was taken into the Bavarian army and issued with Bavarian standards. A cavalry regiment was raised at the same time as that of the infantry, designated as Dragoons and changed to Chevau-Legers in 1812; it was two squadrons strong. Their standard was white in colour and bore on one side the arms of Wurzburg as on the infantry flags. On the other side was the monogram 'F' in gold on a rose pink oval with gold border, laurel and other embroidery. Both sides had a broad gold border. The staffs, like those of the infantry, were red and white spiral-painted. Like the infantry the cavalry regiments were taken into Bavarian service in 1814.

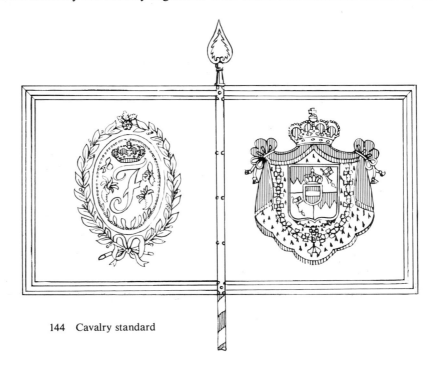

144   Cavalry standard